THE LONG RUN

THE LONG RUN

A MEMOIR OF LOSS AND LIFE IN MOTION

CATRIONA MENZIES-PIKE

CROWN
NEW YORK

Originally published in Australia by Affirm Press, Melbourne, in 2016.

Library of Congress Cataloging-in-Publication Data
Names: Menzies-Pike, Catriona, author.
Title: The Long Run / Catriona Menzies-Pike.
Description: First American Edition. | New York : Crown Publishers,
2017. | Includes bibliographical references.
Identifiers: LCCN 2016040255| ISBN 9781524759445 (hardcover) |
ISBN 9781524759452 (trade pbk.) | ISBN 9781524759469 (E-book)
Subjects: LCSH: Menzies-Pike, Catriona. | Women runners—United
States—Biography. | Runners (Sports)—United States—Biography. |
Running—Health aspects. | Running—United States—History.
Classification: LCC GV1061.15.M47 A3 2017 | DDC 796.42092—dc23
LC record available at https://lccn.loc.gov/2016040255

ISBN 978-1-5247-5944-5
Ebook ISBN 978-1-5247-5946-9

Printed in the United States of America

Book design: Anna Thompson
Jacket design: Michael Morris
Jacket photographs: (woman's head) Andreas Kuehn/Stone/Getty Images;
(runner) PBNJ Productions/Blend Images/Getty Images

10 9 8 7 6 5 4 3 2 1

First American Edition

CONTENTS

THE LONG RUN

INTRODUCTION

I caught a train across the Sydney Harbour Bridge, early one morning in 2013, to run a half marathon. It was chilly, September, and the sky was still a murky gray opal. The carriage buzzed with runners talking the usual nonsense: carb loading, perfect splits, personal bests. Runners can be very annoying en masse.

Three passengers didn't fit in, young men on their way home after a night on the town. They were smashed when they lurched onto the train, the blotto antithesis to all the athletes dressed in spotless, sweat-absorbent shorts and singlets. Something had to give. One of the boozers started to heckle. "Look at you all," he jeered. "What are you doing? Runners! What the fuck are you doing?" On he went. A holy fool in strained black jeans, the young man shook his head in disgust and leaned into a pole for balance, mumbling to himself. I looked down at my shoelaces and lingered on a pang of identification. Imagine, I thought, being stuck in a train full of runners on the way home to a clanging hangover.

Why would anyone run a marathon? Why did you? These aren't inconsequential questions, and I've been fielding them for years now. Intellectual types see marathons as case studies in middle-class sublimation; political activists decry the misdirected energy; relaxed, moderate friends wonder about the showy zealotry of it all. Pretty much everyone who knew me in my sad and reckless twenties has taken me aside to ask why a gin-addled bookworm gave up late nights for long-distance running.

That September morning, all the runners who had been slogging away for months to prepare for their big day pretended not to notice the guy slagging them off—or, should I say, slagging *us* off. When the train stopped, the boozehounds elbowed their way into the morning air. As they wove a course to the exit, the loud one turned back with a last blast. "Why don't one of you fucking idiots do something useful? Write a fucking book." A polite laugh swept over the platform, and we all went off to run 13 miles together.

By the time I boarded that train, I'd read a lot of books about running but I struggled to recognize myself in any of them. They were for people with lives unlike my own: ambitious athletes for whom a marathon time is a measure of self, or obsessives for whom running is the only thing that matters. The motivational sections in bookstores were filled with self-help mantras and sported a dizzying set of bullshitty self-improvement claims: run a marathon to become a better person. The guides for slow runners were waffly exercises in condescension. Not many books about running speak to women, and when they do, it's often about weight loss. As for feminist analyses of running, they were drowned out by exhortations to "run like a girl."

I had come to running relatively late. I didn't even bother to put on my sneakers until I turned thirty. Before that I was the person least likely to run around the block. I'd spent most of my adult life trying to orchestrate circumstances that would allow me to avoid running, and I was happier to wait for the next bus than to chase the one rolling to a stop a block ahead. I rolled my eyes at runners in parks and wondered why any sane woman would put herself through such an ordeal.

I did, however, know all about the desire to run, about endurance and its metaphors. When I was twenty years old, in 1998, my father, who loved running, and my mother, who didn't, died in a plane crash. Life changed, and I found myself with urgent new responsibilities, trying to halt the toxic tailspin of loss. The decade of tears that followed seemed interminable; I stumbled often. I point to that block of sadness when some idiot asks me if this running business is all transference and I'm really running away from the past.

I started running ten years after my parents died, and nothing was as difficult as I'd expected. I found it in myself to move, finally, and experienced that movement not just as liberation, but as transformation. My legs grew strong quickly, and the many pleasures of running through the city were mine; a new geography enveloped me. I'd lived in Sydney for a decade, but I hadn't paid enough attention to the great sweep of coastline and to the open water beyond it. The world changed around me again, more slowly this time.

I found that I had become a runner. Running! Me—a runner! The star of my own one-woman comedy extravaganza. I raved about my discovery to anyone who would listen. "Everybody is identical in their secret unspoken belief that way deep down they are different from everyone else," writes David Foster Wallace in *Infinite Jest*, and when I began to run, I thought I'd hit on something really new. My body was a pendulum, swinging across the landscape; my unlocked limbs tumbled and became light. I learned to feel with my feet, to distinguish between asphalt and concrete beneath my shoes, to love the springiness of wooden decking and the unexpected sink into paths made of shredded tires.

I'm a slow runner, complacent rather than competitive. On a shelf in my study is a scrapbook full of race bibs and a pile of the cheap, chipped medals that every runner is given when she finishes a race. In the beginning, I hung on the advice of a few friends and family members who ran too. My notes seem like fragments of poems that bent my world into a new shape: *Look up the hill. Let yourself float to the top. Find your pace. When you hit that pace, you can run forever.*

Some athletes love to talk about what a simple sport running is. They say that all you need is a pair of sneakers. That's not true. What you need is some freedom of movement and the ability to see a clear path ahead of you. It took me years to see that path and to find my pace. When I finally got moving, I hoped I might be able to run forever.

*

Books shaped my world long before running did. As a child, I squirreled myself away in the library; when I grew up, I wrote a doctoral thesis on modernist literature. Haruki Murakami's memoir *What I Talk about When I Talk about Running* forms a bridge between long-distance running and a certain kind of reading, and I've been given several copies of it. Murakami's title is lifted from a volume of short stories that he translated into Japanese: Raymond Carver's *What We Talk about When We Talk about Love*. Each in their own way, they're books about human endurance. Carver's stories of flight and abandonment explore the sadness, desperation, and hopefulness that compel people to run away from each other—and, sometimes, to return. They leave the reader to deal with a thick residue of melancholy. When Carver's characters talk about love, what they're really talking about is hate and resentment and loss; when Murakami talks about running, he's actually talking about the life of a writer.

Stories about running are often like this, in that they're about something else. They are tales of shape-shifting, of the desire to shed one skin and step into another. One running story may be a parable on persistence or denial; another a warning. It took more than running, of course, for me to haul myself out of the quicksand of grief. But the practice helped me rewrite the script I'd been following and craft a new set of stories about enduring, flight, and change.

The position of the foot distinguishes running from walking. Walkers always have one foot on the ground and runners always have one foot off it. That's simple enough, but the word *run* is a case study in linguistic locomotion: it flows and moves, changing its subjects and controlling its objects. Blood runs cold, rivers run, bulls run through the streets, dye runs in the wash, chills run down the spine, stockings run after a night out dancing. *Running* is easy to modify: it can be a messenger for functionality, *running in good order*; for dissipation, *running to seed*; for depletion, *running on empty*; and for abundance, *my cup runneth over*. The quick, slippery movement of the word *run*—verb and noun, process and thing, inspiration and accomplishment—points to the complex interactions between runners' bodies and minds. Persistence, endurance, and resilience can each be expressed through the language of running. As a result of this dexterity, running is an astonishingly variable metaphor for the inner life.

To map the meaning of any kind of run, we need to pay attention to prepositions. A tale about running away from home follows a different itinerary from one about running back home. The language of running is gendered too. As I ran more, I began to listen closely to the inflections that distinguish cautionary tales about women runners from heroic epics about the men who run after them. Subjects versus objects: one runner might experience the thrill of the chase; the other, the terror of being chased.

Running changed the stories I could tell about myself, finally: I had a new theme, and it didn't turn on misfortune. *The Strange True Tale of an Unlikely Runner.* "No, no, it's not that dangerous if you run slowly," I told the people who were worried about my joints. *Getting over Grief, Getting on the Road.* "You just keep running, one foot in front of the other," is what I said to the people who wanted to know how I did it. *How Gertrude Stein Helped Me Go the Distance.* When I saw old friends,

I had good news, for once: "You won't believe it, I've started running." *From Martinis to Marathons: How I Kicked the Gloom and Crossed the Finish Line.* When people professed their admiration, I played it down: "I didn't break any records, but if I can do it, anyone can." *Freak Out: Library Lizard Joins the Jocks.*

Nothing of my surprise conversion to running was reflected in the books I read on the topic, so I wrote this one. A personal history that relies on a wayward account of women's long-distance running, one that gives runners like me a bit of room to move: slow runners, unambitious runners, antisocial runners. I look at the language that is used to talk about women runners and the stories that get told about them, whether they're fast or slow. Of course, not every reader will recognize herself in these pages.

Gender is one lens through which we can look at people running, and that's the approach I've taken here. The website *Stuff White People Like*, a satirical guide to white middle-class manners, includes an entry on marathons: "Running for a certain length of time on a specific day is a very important thing to a white person and should not be demeaned." There's another book to be written on how race and class affect our perception of bodies in motion, and still others that place global justice, sexuality, disability, and trans issues at center stage.

This book draws on what I already knew about literature, about feminist politics, and about endurance, as much as it taps the wisdom of training guides, hot runners, and tough coaches. In every way, *The Long Run* is shaped by the lives I've lived before and beyond running: by the dorky little kid who took remedial throw-and-catch classes, by the wide-eyed undergraduate with a nose ring who had to grow up overnight, by the barfly who grimaced at the morning joggers, by the feminist who wouldn't leave it alone, and by the reader who preferred to retreat into fictions. It's taken me thousands of miles to write.

1

MAKING A SCENE

On a cold night in early May, a Saturday, I stood in a park with six thousand women. We were all wearing the same dark pink singlet. As we shivered under the bright lights, two clowns in heavy jackets and winter beanies bopped around on a stage and barked commendations into microphones. *Ladies, you all look so hot. You girls are amazing. You got yourselves here tonight and that's a huge achievement. Give yourselves a massive cheer!* The party music didn't stop for a beat. That particular shade of pink, a late-night raspberry with a hint of blood, is one of my favorite colors, and I resented having to share it with so many people.

I was waiting to start the 2014 Nike-sponsored She Runs event in Sydney's Centennial Park, a 10-kilometer, women-only night run. The words *She Runs SYD* were printed at nipple-height on our six thousand pink singlets: no one could possibly forget where we were and why we were here. No event singlet, no run. *Sorry ladies, those are the rules.* I had everything that it took to fit in: a singlet, a gender identity and a willingness to run 10 kilometers in the dark.

If you've never mustered with thousands of people at the start of a running race, you won't be familiar with the encouragements that are bellowed into these crowds. At She Runs the Night, the script had been tweaked to suit women runners. *All of you at the back of the pack, give yourselves a huge cheer. Let's hear it for the first-timers! Anyone here from out of town? Come on, give them a cheer! And let's hear it for the mums! You've all made it to the starting line, so you're all winners to me.* I'd run in scores of races, and should have been used to this relentless bonhomie.

The beginning of any big run is intimate and slightly awkward. Nervous strangers are squashed into a small space to wait for the starting gun, sometimes for hours. It's more common to gather in the early morning, close enough to other runners to inspect their tan lines, tattoos, scars, and scabs in the half-light. That May night was unexpectedly cold, and the floodlights picked out goose bumps on the women around me. Some hugged themselves and jumped on the spot, others danced in front of a friend's camera or turned cartwheels under a disco ball.

At this bright, noisy threshold, I had no hope of accessing the steady roaming headspace that I reach when running alone. That's what I love most about running—but without races like She Runs on my calendar, I'd probably slack off on the training, even though I know how exhilarating it can be. And so, despite my ambivalence about the crowds and the fuss and the motivational claptrap, my running career has been al-most entirely structured by events like these.

"You know, I'm not really into sports," I recently reminded a friend who'd invited me to a cricket match. "Yes, you are," he said. "You've got your running." If this claim that I don't really fit in with the running scene keeps me going, over the years I've had to accept that it's not completely true. I've grown used to the carnival of the starting line. I wish I had a story to tell about running that didn't involve goons with megaphones and party crowds. I wish I didn't need a race looming to convince me to get up early and go for a run—but I do. And so I keep finding myself in places like this, fighting the instinct to elbow a path to the perimeter, beyond the range of the strobe lights and the amp, and then to hop over the railings and bolt home.

I'd never run in a women-only event before and I hoped that night to encounter something new at She Runs. One aspect of the event was distinctive: it was pink. Shockingly pink. Ma-genta, fluorescent pink, cutie-pie baby pink, stripper pink, and every shade of princess pink that's ever tinted a plastic hairclip. Pink neon lights stretched over the stage. A floodlight swept through the crowd, picking out shining, happy faces and pink, slippery shirts. Glowing tubes were bent around scaffolds as if to convince us that the lights were held up by musk sticks. Stalls selling shoes and sports drinks were festooned with pink fairy lights. A tour de force of monochrome branding. The starting line hadn't been sluiced with pink only to dazzle and seduce us—it effectively conscripted every raspberry-singleted woman as an extra in the show. Above us floated drones fitted with cameras, as if we were performers in a song-and-dance spectacular.

Only runners were permitted in this pink arena, designated the "event village." Supporters had been banished to the other side of the barriers. An event village might sound cozy, but really it was just a set of stalls, stages, and scaffolds standing in what the day before had been an open patch of parkland. Security guards held the barricades, their nightclub schtick ludicrous: "Pink singlet? In you go." In spite of the party trappings, the village wasn't a space of gleeful exclusion, one freed from the inhibitions and restrictions of everyday life. No, it was much more like a tiny Swiss municipality, complete with service infrastructure and many rules: first-aid officers and ambulances stood at the ready, and so did Nike sales reps. Event officials in safety vests and ask-me-anything smiles fielded questions about public toilets and water bottles.

Flashes and cheers ricocheted around the event village. A huge screen loomed over the stage, and several more hung high from a pink scaffold. The most impressive was the selfie tower, its four faces representing the northern, southern, eastern, and western suburbs of Sydney. Four queues of excited women and girls spiraled around this tower, new communities created by running bodies. If their pics were marked with the right hashtag, they were projected onto one of the screens. Photos of women in pink singlets scrolled by: Pymble girls, Shire girls, #northsidecrew, Bondi legends, Bankstown legends, Penrith runners, Katoomba runners, on it went. *We want to hear you girls make some noise when you see your selfie*, said the hucksters with the microphones. *Let everyone know you're having the time of your life!*

This was the third year that a She Runs event had been held in Sydney; similar women-only night runs stamped with Nike swooshes are held all over the world. The emphasis is firmly on inclusion and participation, rather than aggressive competition. *You should totally do it*, friends told me. *You love running.* They were right—a night like She Runs should have been just my thing. And yet, why did it have to be a reiteration of the thesis that ladies love pink? What happened in the marketing meeting that turned a running event into a glorified shoe sale? Maybe I'd forgotten how to have fun. But who'd made the decision to give a pair of sexist dirtbags the microphone at a women-only event? I was irked by their assurances that we were all beautiful and amazing and really, really hot. I just wanted to get on with it.

*

The day hadn't begun auspiciously. It was raining when I woke up. Big races require participants to pick up a "race pack" in the week before the event: essentially showbags that are packed with advertising guff, samples of new products for amateur athletes—maybe a sachet of sunscreen or a can of electrolytes—as well as vital items such as timing chips and, in this instance, the pink singlet. Carrying a race pack around is a quick way to signal that you're a runner. In six years of running, I'd amassed a pretty good collection of them. This time, however, I'd neglected to pick up my race pack and now, to retrieve it, not only would I get a scolding from irritated officials, I'd also get drenched.

Home and dry, I ate a late lunch and flicked through the running magazine that had been shoved into the pack, seeking some last-minute training advice. *Be thin. Be strong. Be sexy. Be in control. Do it your way. Let yourself lose control. Live a little. Have it all. Eat more carbs, more protein. Fill up on good fats. Love yourself, but don't slack off. Watch out for avocados. Treat yourself sometimes. Wonderfoods, superfoods. Five-minute ab revolutions. New shoes might put the spring back in your step. Romance at the gym. Free workouts.* There were so many rules, so many exceptions to the rules. I lacked the dexterity to dodge the cuts and thrusts. And so, rolling my eyes, I chucked the magazine into my recycling pile.

The rain finally stopped, and I marched through the twilight to Centennial Park. I'd been warned that the event village gates would shut early—if I didn't appear on time, wearing my uniform, I wouldn't be allowed to run. These are the injunctions delivered to schoolgirls, not to grown women. I'd layered up: running shorts over leggings, a slippery long-sleeved shirt under my pink singlet. Neither flattering nor comfortable, but I knew that I'd stay warm.

I felt extremely foolish, but I kept going because I was drawn to the idea of a women-only event. I wondered how it might be different to run in this crowd. The magazine hadn't given me much cause for optimism, but I hoped that some shared experiences might not, for once, be left unspoken. I can't remember exactly what I was anticipating. Breasts, bras, bleeding, and babies? Hardly. Would a feminist trailblazer be called up to lead us on our way and inspire us to pick up the pace? Maybe the organizers would be bold enough to acknowledge the lived experiences of trans women. I hoped, I suppose, that the event would at least be free of catcalling and pervy bystanders.

I also hoped that the sense of uneasiness that so many women feel when running in public spaces—especially alone, especially after dark—would somehow be suspended. Running in the dark piqued my interest. I would never run in Centennial Park on my own at night. Years ago, I sometimes cut through the park on my bike after midnight, taking a route home from the pub that mostly wasn't illumined by streetlights. I was more reckless then, and still it frightened me. I'd grip the handlebars tightly and stare into the short wan beam of my headlight, hoping its batteries would hold out. I told myself that possums were responsible for the shuffling and grumbling in the bushes, and chastised myself for not having taken the longer, well-lit path, even if there were more cars and hills to deal with. Every time I left the park at the Oxford Street gates, I exhaled the tension, shrugged my shoulders, and resolved never to take that path again.

On morning runs, I have occasionally followed a dirt and sand track that hugs the perimeter of Centennial Park, encountering only a few dog walkers and other runners. Usually it's spookily quiet, a surprising contrast to the packed main paths of the park. I'd be overstating it if I said that I've felt in peril on that sandy track in the early morning, but I am acutely aware of my surroundings there. I get a jittery sense of confinement in sections with a high fence on one side and high shrubs on the other, and mild alarm strikes when the path is too twisty and overgrown to give me a strong sense of who might be approaching. Do I expect belligerent strangers to leap out of the bushes? Perhaps. I grasp at the hope that I'm fit enough and fast enough to run away from anyone now—and that the park is full of friendly people. Whenever another lone runner crosses my path, we exchange greetings, maybe a wave, and carry on. I still often find myself uncomfortable when alone in poorly lit, depthless places like these. And that's why, in spite of all the pink neon, I was excited to see the park full of people, to see the space cordoned off for a safe communal activity.

Centennial Park is the largest urban park in Sydney. When it opened in 1888, no one would have dreamed that six thousand women might gather to run its circuit, let alone in the dark. Women running for any reason other than to get out of trouble is an extraordinarily recent phenomenon—not that you'd know it under the pink lights. It's a shock to discover that only a few decades ago, a women-only distance run would have been highly controversial. In fact, the history of running is shaped by ancient anxieties about women on the move and stern prohibitions on where they could go. The road for today's women runners was first trodden by brave, rebellious athletes a few generations older than me. They broke rules and bothered race officials, sports commentators, their fathers, moralizing tut-tutters, and many other women. Now the objections that were, not so long ago, raised to women running even 10 kilometers—it's unladylike, it might affect fertility, it might stimulate weight loss, it's altogether silly—sound preposterous. She Runs is a very well-groomed and well-behaved culmination of this history. That I heard no one mention the past was at least, I told myself, a sign that it had been left behind.

*

The title "She Runs the Night" makes the event sound a lot like another gathering of women, Reclaim the Night, and its American sister, Take Back the Night. These explicitly feminist events also involve women and girls taking to public spaces after dark—but marching down streets, not running around parks, in the name of safety for women. When I joined these marches in the late 1990s and the early 2000s, they were lit with candles rather than neon tubes.

It's thrilling to venture into public places that are normally decreed out of bounds. Protesters and runners both get the chance to take over the roads on foot, sending vehicles into exile. When I first ran in road races, I was vividly reminded of the wonderful city views I'd enjoyed when protests took me off the sidewalk and onto the pavement. Familiar sights are transformed when viewed from the center of the road. Anyone who's been scared walking home alone at night can understand how powerful it is to fill dark streets with light and exuberant human bodies.

I've still got a calico bag from a late-1990s Reclaim the Night march, which now stores obsolete computer cables and plugs. (If the She Runs carry bag lasts as long, I'll be impressed.) The image on the speckled cream fabric is printed in purple ink, of course. When I tip out the junk and smooth the bag on the carpet, I see a woman with Medusa dreads wearing a kaftan and playing a drum, blissed out on the beats, her eyes closed. Next to her is a woman with Gloria Steinem glasses, striped pants, and a guitar. The Harbour Bridge grins in the background. There's also a ballerina, a woman in a wheelchair with spiky hair and a choker, a woman in a daisy-printed waistcoat with her hair cropped short. Everyone is smiling and holding candles, and someone has brought a confused-looking cat and dog to the party. You can almost smell the nag champa in the air.

I have to be honest: the bag is an incredibly dorky artifact from feminist history, all right-on hairy armpits, bongos, and menstrual dirges. The kind of clichés that I think make young women who are invested in equal pay, safety from violence, and reproductive rights tell journalists that they don't actually see themselves as feminists. Markers of identity are rendered in thick, earnest strokes. It's hard to detect any cultural diversity. I think the short-haired women are supposed to be lesbians. In these days of intersectional, trans-positive feminism, the bag strikes me as a friendly but very unsophisticated map of feminist community.

In the battle over visual identity, Nike clearly has the upper hand. Everywhere I looked at She Runs, I saw slick branding. Pink cranes held bright Nike swooshes aloft. Cheerful PR assistants wore backpacks to which floating, logo-printed balloons were tethered. There were long lines for the enormous inflated trampoline, another unmissable selfie opportunity. The night was a virtuoso demonstration of the marketing sleight of hand that turns participation into consumption. Every image was designed to reassure participants that we were sexy, modern, and cool. I drafted lines for the twerps onstage: *We're not here for politics, we're here to pa-a-arty.*

As unstylish as they might have been, it was in earnest and optimistic environments such as Reclaim the Night that I formed my ideas about gender and politics. They made me a feminist long before I was a runner. And so, to me, efforts to separate one section of the community—women, say—from the rest, whether for profit or protest, are inherently political.

It bothered me that I didn't hear one word from that pink stage about street safety, about how frightening big parks can feel to women alone at night, how crowds can share not just fun, but also solidarity. No one asked questions about the category of woman or made gestures of inclusion to trans women. If there was a welcome that acknowledged Indigenous women, I missed it. Not a word about sexual harassment, or income disparity, or domestic violence. What a downer that would have been. It was just a group of women running in a brightly lit park on a Saturday night, their menfolk relegated to the sidelines. Everyone around me was having a great time. What's political about that? Grumbling away in the crowd on my own, I didn't feel like an edgy feminist critic; I felt like the odd one out.

*

When I tell people that women didn't run the Olympic marathon before 1984, that women weren't allowed to run more than 800 meters at the Olympic level until 1960, they're incredulous. It's such a tangible exhibit of sexism. *But you run,* they cry, *even you!* How could it be that women weren't even allowed to enter 10-kilometer events? The "natural" order changes fast.

Women runners now enjoy a visible culture of participation and inclusion, and sponsors like Nike have played an important role in promoting this. They've sold a lot of shoes and shorts in whatever shade of tough pink or assertive gray the season favors—and, on the way, they've helped to normalize women's recreational running. When events like She Runs were first organized in the early 1970s, most sports officials were digging in to defend the idea that even elite female athletes shouldn't run long distances.

The first official women's marathon took place in 1973, in West Germany, and the first international women's marathon was held there the following year. These events utterly confounded the conventional wisdom about women runners. As the '70s got underway, so did women-only distance events—such as the Crazylegs Mini Marathon in New York in 1972, a 10-kilometer run hosted by the New York City Marathon founder and race director Fred Lebow. The event was named after the sponsor's product, a brand of shaving gel for women. The Bonne Bell Mini Marathon series started in the United States in 1977, another 10-kilometer event. By 1978, the Avon International Women's Marathon Series was underway too. Over the next eight years, two hundred women-only marathons were raced under the Avon banner in twenty-seven countries.

That cosmetics companies—the purveyors of shiny lips and glossy pins—were among the key enablers of women's running seems a little less incongruous in the girlie party zone at the starting line of She Runs. Corporate-sponsored, women-only events are now a fixture of the running circuit and have fostered several generations of women runners with the promise of safe, hassle-free spaces to run.

Equal running rights for all isn't the catchphrase of a politically radical movement. When women weren't allowed to run long distances in the late 1960s and the early '70s, campaigners made a straightforward liberal case for equal treatment. They weren't trying to change the world; they just wanted to run in it. That said, the campaign to allow women access to the Olympic marathon played out in parallel to broader feminist battles over the body. Women wanted sexual freedom, reproductive freedom, access to the workplace—as well as the right to run long distances. In providing a set of new stories about strength, speed, and resilience, the women's running movement was a powerful repudiation of patriarchal claims about women's bodies: one of the reasons why those guys onstage, going on about how hot we were, got on my nerves.

There's a big difference between access to safe, legal abortion and being able to wear a pink singlet that identifies you as a paid-up entrant in a running race, but they both involve women having a say about what our bodies can do. Being able to run in parks without fear of molestation, whether that's to train for a marathon or to get a bit fitter, is part of a bigger freedom to be safe in both public and private places. The decision to run 5 or 10 or 20 miles is a recognition that our bodies are our own, and that we can choose how far we run, whom we sleep with, what we eat, whether or not to take a pregnancy to term, and how we might swing our arms and legs to take us through our days.

All this might have seemed a bit heavy in that pink arena, were it not that "She Runs the Night" sounds like a feminist slogan, and the organizers were making us wait out in the cold for what seemed an unnecessarily long time.

*

We didn't all start to run at once. No, the women of She Runs were to cross the starting line in orderly waves. We'd been invited to seed ourselves according to how long we thought it would take us to complete the course. There was no need to rush or to push when our wave was called, we were assured. We were all chipped, we'd all be individually timed, and anyway, this wasn't a race, it was an event, and we were all participants, running with and not against each other. As we waited, the runners in the green wave were called to cheer for their group, and then the red wave, then the purple, and so on. In this state of perpetual encouragement, you might even let yourself believe that a level playing field could yield equal outcomes. God forbid we see each other as competitors.

I'd predicted a sedate time for myself but, even so, I spent much more time waiting to start than I did actually running. Training runs are nothing like this—it's off and away, immediately. I watched the crowd as I waited, and I wondered at its identities. What stories might the people around me tell about their lives and their running if I got them at the right moment? That trio of twenty-three-year-olds with matching pearl earrings—were they schoolmates or had they grown into versions of each other working together? I was too shy to interrupt their giggling and ask, "Why are you here?" like some two-bit workshop leader. Maybe they played on a sports team together and decided this would be a fun way to cap off the season. Maybe a friend had died and they were raising money in her memory. And the woman in her mid-forties with huge burnished muscles wrapped round her arms and a full face of makeup, what drew her to this race? One of the few loners I spotted, she looked like she could run 50 miles and wrestle a python. What did I know—maybe she managed a women's health center.

In that crowd, there must have been mothers, lesbians, rich women, poor women, trans women, single women, women who ran five miles five times a week, and women who hoped to run the distance for the first time. Some must have been dragged there by friends or sisters. There were probably a few who, like me, had turned up out of an intermingled sense of curiosity and gender solidarity, a sense that if you're going to join any running crowd, it might as well be a crowd of women. I was so engrossed in these reflections that I jumped like a bird when a young woman asked me to help her attach a timing strip to her shoe.

Looking back, what's really amazing is that I had the emotional energy to grumble about the usurpation of a particular shade of pink by a corporation—that I hadn't blown it all on worrying about whether I could run 10 kilometers. I'd become so used to running that I was wondering how many in the crowd were single, instead of flipping out about the distance. In my first races, a more immediate self-absorption prevailed, and it still does over longer distances. I worry about collapsing in knots of muscle pain and dehydration, about tripping on my shoelaces and being too tired to stop myself from falling; I used to worry about being able to finish the race.

I learned to calm myself down with the clichés about individual endeavor that are the natural language of amateur athletes. *Just run your own race*, I made my inner coach say. *Relax, enjoy the atmosphere and take your time.* Somehow I found a kind of confidence. I stopped seeing myself as a hopeless case, an injury risk, a likely dropout, and started seeing myself as a runner. Running transformed me from someone who was terrified of long distances into a woman possessed of the happy certainty that she could run 10 kilometers and then walk home to complain about the pinkification of feminist politics.

How far is 10 kilometers? A lap of a typical track is 400 meters. Four laps (plus 9 meters) is a mile. To run 10 kilometers you need to make it around that oval twenty-five times. At school, I hated running around the track more than any other activity; then, I could have imagined no greater abjection than long-distance running. To a super-fit endurance athlete, 10 kilometers is nothing. It isn't much of a training run. To a natural athlete, possessed of good coordination and enviable confidence, 10 kilometers is a manageable distance, one that doesn't require any particularly rigorous training. To someone who doesn't run, it's a hell of a long way.

That night, I knew my legs could take me 10 kilometers, farther if I wanted them to. I had planned a longer solo run a day or two after the race, and could have run 10 kilometers anywhere in the city on that rainy Saturday. I stayed because I wanted to find out what it was like to run in a crowd of women. I stayed because these experiences of being in a mass of runners, even as they irritate me, remind me of all the ways that my life has changed, that even the most unlikely scenes can yield possibility.

Running has a way of dragging you into the present moment of exertion. In those early races, when I was worrying about my calves seizing up, the attention I devoted to the sensations between my knees and my ankles made me forget about any other concerns I had to lug around. At She Runs, the present moment was pink and loud and bright, and as the shuffle toward the starting line finally gave way to running, I relaxed into the fizz of the crowd.

The first stretch was a narrow chute tightly packed with sharp elbows, along which I hopped and skittered, looking for clear space to move. The course widened, and we left the lights behind. In the darkness I found a rhythm. I wriggled my toes to feel the bounce as my feet left the ground. My heart rate picked up, and the real warmth of movement flowed through my limbs. As my shoulders loosened, I pulled my head up higher to better take in the crowd.

Other women were realigning their bodies to fit into the space, as pleased as I was finally to be moving. Was it the reliable endorphin hit that made me smile at this scene? If we had nothing else to share, we had the same finish line in sight. I waved at the kids who were huddled on the sidelines waiting for their mothers to pass by. I got dizzy running through a stretch of the park lit by a spinning disco ball, then was surprised by darkness—at one point, when I looked down, I couldn't quite make out my feet. I slowed down and placed each foot carefully, worried that I might trip over my shoes or skid on a loose rock.

I ended where I'd started, in the candy-cane event village. This is how most running stories end, back at the beginning. And yet, I carry with me—and so does everyone, I think, who crosses a finish line—the sense that something momentous has taken place. Running through the final colonnade decked with Nike flags, I heard someone blurt out a triumphant, "Yes!" It could have been anyone. To finish a race, even slowly, even under pink lights, even when you harbor no doubts about being able to complete the distance, is a fine feeling. The run had lifted my mood—but not enough for me to join the awesome pink party. I cut a path across a section of the park that hadn't been lit up, and when I reached the gate, I turned back to watch the lights of that one-night-only running utopia flicker, knowing that next time I visited the park, all traces of the event would have disappeared.

2

ON THE TREADMILL

I'd like to be able to claim that I started running with one great, effortless reflex, that I sat bolt upright in bed one morning with a resolution to start running, that I pulled on a pair of sneakers and tumbled down a joyful path to the park at the end of my street, that I ran through a screen separating the runners of this world from the nonrunners, and emerged an electrified body, springing ecstatic between the earth and sky. That all came much later. The truth is, I started running on a treadmill in the back corner of a grimy Sydney gym.

The treadmill was invented to punish prisoners with work. Inmates in nineteenth-century prisons around the world walked on treadmills for hours to grind grain. Prison supervisors reported that the repetitive exertion also ground down morale, and so ensured that the prison population remained docile, or, failing that, just exhausted. Not all prisons used their treadmills to process grain—some set prisoners to walk for hours as mindless, pointless punishment.

Gyms are where such futile exertions are restaged, only with consent and for a fee. If one were, in a moment of disquiet, to launch a diatribe about what's wrong with wealthy Western cities, a gym would be a good spot to start: in gyms it is possible to observe the most debased expressions of contemporary ideas about the body, work, pleasure, and leisure. Wooden banter about everyday masochism—punishing yourself with a workout, penance for caloric splurges—is built into the discourse of self-improvement. To me, those rows of cardio machines, facing screens tuned to tranquilizing television, look like props for a giant dystopian con. I know gyms are standard destinations—*everyone goes to the gym these days*—but until I started running, I would have dismissed as ridiculous the notion that a gym might serve as a refuge.

I walked into that gym in Kings Cross months after declaring to my family that I would someday run a marathon. When I first stepped onto a treadmill, running a marathon was a bizarre and distant fantasy. I loathed running, but something about the idea of running long distances had lodged in my imagination. I was drawn to the theory and so, in what still seems an astounding suspension of long-held views on exertion, I decided to give the practice a go.

I'd just returned home from a long year of aimless travel, and I was very unfit and still aimless. I set upon a modest goal: to complete the City2Surf, a 14-kilometer (8.7-mile) run from the center of Sydney to Bondi Beach. It's hard now to explain just how unlikely this scenario was. I doubted I'd stick with my gym membership, let alone enter the race. Would I actually run it? Any gambler who knew my previous form would have held on to her dough. Until now I'd complained vehemently about the noise and inconvenience this race generated, especially to inner-city residents like me. Why would I cast myself into a pit of unreconstructed running evangelists, and align myself with the joggers who made waiting for coffee on the sidewalk so hazardous? I didn't let these questions get under my skin. The starting date was months away, and I was as used to abandoning my plans as I was to making them.

*

And so I started running at the gym when I was thirty, plugged into a treadmill like a subject in an experiment titled "The Effects of Exercise on Depressed, Unhealthy People." Really, though, the story of why I started running, and why the discovery of movement was such a revelation, has deeper roots. For ten years, my life had been stuck still, immobilized even, by loss.

When I was twenty, I wasn't thinking about running. I was an undergraduate at Sydney University, deliriously happy to be living in the city, to be an inhabitant of that careless, liminal state between adolescence and adulthood. I was marching in anti-Nike protests and smoking rollies on the balcony of Manning Bar. Treadmills, I would have insisted, were a technology of self-loathing, an instrument of the patriarchal control of women's bodies. Treadmills? I wanted roller coasters, magic carpets, teleporters, time machines. It was a moment for manifestos and declarations. My parents worried that I was becoming strident—"bolshy" was my father's preferred appellation—but they left me to grow up on my own terms. If my tone is nostalgic, that's because that irretrievable time, being twenty years old, represents the point just before my life was upended. Until then, my days were full of the uplifting possibilities of being young and, although I didn't really understand it, loved, and safe.

And then, one Sunday, my three younger sisters and I received news that a plane carrying my parents and four of their friends had gone missing. They had flown to the coast for a weekend away, in a little Cessna that belonged to one of their group, an experienced pilot who was in the cockpit. To celebrate submitting an essay, I'd taken myself to the Blue Mountains for a day of solo hiking. My housemates had fielded phone calls from family friends all afternoon but I was oblivious to anything but the autumn sun and the train timetable. None of us had cell phones then; I'd spent the day truly away, watching skinks play under waterfalls. I arrived home to my shocked friends and this prospect that was just too gigantic to credit. A plane crash? That night, I flew home to Albury, the town where I'd grown up. It seemed like an overreaction.

The next morning, just after nine, a young policewoman knocked on the glass front door of our family home to break the news. I remember her mousy hair and how terribly nervous she was. My sisters had taken the day off school. Dad should have been at work, asking questions about someone's rickety hip, hitting some kid's knee with a hammer. If it had been a normal day, he would already have been up for hours. A person possessed of formidable energy and self-discipline, my father expected others to share his enthusiasm for work. It was autumn, too cold for kayaking, so he would have gone for a run or hopped on his bike. He should have caught up on the medical reports that he always seemed to need to write, or watched a gory, unrated video of a procedure that he'd have to perform later that day. My parents, Jane and Ian, were both doctors. They'd fallen in love in their first year of medical school, married on graduation, raised four daughters, and never separated. Mum was an early riser too. She would have taken the dogs out into the brisk morning for a walk, fussed in the garden, read the newspaper looking out for the names of people she knew in town.

They seemed to me terribly conservative and settled. I was primed for cosmopolitan adventure: graduate school in New York or London; the life of a crusading lawyer, perhaps; bars in Tangier and Montevideo; transcontinental train travel, rickety ferries, reckless journeys; daring literary feats, scandals, even; many lovers, brilliant friends; worthy environmental crusades, no compromises; ruins, art, literature, rebellion, revolution, the usual. Like many other undergraduates from fortunate homes, my aspirations could be summed up in a few words: not being like my parents.

On a normal morning, Mum and Dad would have shared breakfast before my sisters had rolled out of bed. Instead, Lucy, Claudia, Laura, and I were sitting on a couch surrounded by adults who should have been at work. The report on the search for the missing plane was on the front page of the local newspaper and it was already out of date. The plane had been found in the Jagungal Wilderness, the policewoman told us, and there were no survivors. It had hit the ground, that same newspaper reported the next day, "like a frozen brick." The policewoman burst into tears, and so did everybody else in the room.

There was no space for a nicely organized five-step grieving process, for a regulated passage from denial to acceptance. It was the wrong kind of pain, the wrong kind of loss for a twenty-year-old arts student. I was geared for heartbreak, artistic self-righteousness, political protest—not this. Whatever structure our lives had, it collapsed. Anyone who has read a book of fairy tales knows that orphans have a hard time. My sisters and I were terribly vulnerable to the cruel, and also to the curious. Shock quickly gave way to responsibility.

I'd already moved out of the house and was the only one who looked like an adult, and that, barely. Laura was thirteen, Claudia was fifteen, and Lucy was eighteen and finishing her last year of school. I'd shaved my head the year before in an act of feminist defiance. That was now juvenilia. I had a major in semiotics and was writing an honors thesis on the prosody of the American poet Marianne Moore. Now people were asking me questions such as, *Where will the family live? What will you do with the house? Who will take care of your mother's roses?* In many families faced with a dreadful situation like this, the responsibility of caring for the younger siblings would have fallen on the eldest. The guardian named in my parents' will wasn't much help, but generous family friends, truly the best of people, made it possible for my sisters to finish high school and for me to continue with my studies part-time.

We didn't always make the right decisions, but we managed to work out a path from week to week. My sisters have their own stories about that time, and they're not mine to tell. I kept my room in Glebe with my beloved housemates, and ping-ponged between Sydney and Albury weekly at first, then fortnightly. I had plenty of time to read on the train. The treadmill is sometimes used as a metaphor for dead-end jobs or relationships, for scenarios in which people work hard and get nowhere. That's what this felt like.

*

I became very familiar with the rhythms of the night train that still leaves Central Station soon after eight o'clock and arrives in Albury in the darkest hours of the morning. One autumn night, just shy of a year after the plane crash, I'd told a friend of my parents not to pick me up from the station. It wasn't far, and I could walk, I assured her, or just catch a taxi home. I didn't want to inconvenience her. The kindness we'd been shown felt like a staggering burden, a debt we'd never be able to repay. And anyway, I wanted to appear independent, to show that I was surviving.

Country towns are horribly quiet in the early morning, and I listened to my footsteps echoing through the wide streets as I walked home. My parents would not have approved. A clock chimed three times, and I jumped in fright. It was cold and dark when I arrived at the gate of our empty house. Nobody had lived there for months.

I was exhausted, but when I tried to open the back door, my key didn't work. No one had told me that the locks had been changed. I climbed into the garden and tracked a path around the house looking for open windows, but they all had new locks too. I couldn't even jimmy the window of my childhood bedroom as I'd done so many times in high school.

I stood in the sheltered area by a door, wondering what the hell I was going to do. A car pulled up in the driveway and paused, headlights blazing on the other side of the gate. The arrival terrified me. Had someone seen me walking home alone? Everyone in town knew that our house was empty. I drew myself out of sight and waited until the car drove off. The next morning I discovered that it was the woman who'd offered me the lift: she'd wanted to make sure I arrived home safely.

I was too tired and too rattled and too cold to pace Albury's empty streets alone until dawn. Instead, I folded myself into a shivering ball on the doormat beside the back door of the house, pulled all the clothes out of my travel bag, tucked my jeans and T-shirts around me, and waited for the light.

I was awakened by a neighbor who'd come over to check on something, I forget what, and found me under a pile of clothes on the step. I woke up, stiff, dusty, dirty. He thought I was a homeless person, and I could see that he was readying himself to make a speech. I stood up, shedding my makeshift blankets, and hurried to explain. He recognized me then, that this was my home, or at least had been, and neither of us knew what to say.

*

Plane crash, both parents, younger sisters, orphans: these were components of a story I didn't yet understand. I'd just started to find my own identity, and now I was defined as my parents' daughter all over again.

It's not so bad, I told myself. I learned how to preempt questions from new acquaintances and colleagues about my family, to manage their distress and awkwardness and pity. I got used to hearing about people's fear of flying. Polished stories and a slightly distant manner are helpful shields to hide behind when your life has been broken in such an obvious fashion; it's not possible to be emotionally authentic with every stranger or friend who asks, *Where do your parents live? Are you going home for Christmas? Is that your mother's smile? Who are these people in the photograph? Do you ever really get the feeling that your parents don't understand who you are?*

Terrible things happen in this world, I made myself say. In some ways, we're lucky—and we were, insofar as we were on safe ground financially. I knew we were protected by money and I knew godawful things happened to others who didn't have this cushion. I volunteered in community legal centers where I heard aching stories about lives in crisis. Some people let my sisters and me down terribly—but we had good friends who helped us survive. It could be worse, I reminded myself, but actually, this was the worst thing that had ever happened to me.

Nothing sprang back into shape. The great catastrophe of my parents' deaths was followed by other setbacks. It would take a different book to itemize the sadness and stress of those first years after Mum and Dad died; everything was immeasurably worse because we had to cope without them. There were years of unhappy wrangling with the insurers of the plane. The changed locks were a premonition of what was to come: difficulties with the executorship of my parents' will escalated quickly and ultimately took legal intervention to settle, amid much ill feeling and misunderstanding. Behind the bolted doors, our family home fell into empty disrepair. People who wanted to help were scared away, and the broader family circle was torn.

My mother's mother was stunned by the death of her only

child. She died of a broken heart a few years after her daughter. Disoriented, my sisters and I took our bearings from a few adults: our grandfather, our wonderful aunt Anne, a loyal cluster of family friends in Albury. We were welcome in many houses but, still, we had lost our home and our center.

My recollection of this time isn't complete. The dates and years blur into one another. I didn't take many photographs and kept gloomy journals only sporadically. I struggled too to remember who my parents were. Memories of a halcyon *before* seemed like snapshots of someone else's life. I remember my sisters and I teasing my father when he brought home fancy new cycling gear, flashy bright lycra togs that didn't match his personality. His moods were hard to discern, but in this moment we are eating breakfast in the kitchen, there are yellow flowers on the curtains, sun streams through the window like a flare, and my father is laughing with his daughters. Such memories are shot through with a warm light, and we all move fluidly, as if there's nothing to resist. It was a happy, comfortable house; the snags and whorls of family life just sink into that mellow glow.

Such half-truths and distortions are the kinder deceptions of grief. In this light, my mother is glamorous. If her emphasis on appropriate dress once frustrated me, now it is her soft red sweaters, beautiful creamy shirts, dark, rustling evening gowns, which she had few occasions to wear, that I remember. Her silk scarves were always ironed, her silver necklaces and brooches were always polished, and I, her eldest daughter, worried her terribly by letting my hair get ratty and insisting on grubby secondhand clothes. I can't see her running; she preferred to amble, to chat, to see what was blooming in the gardens on her route. It took years for me to realize that my parents might have astounded me, that the lives they would have led after their daughters grew up and left home might have been nothing like those they did lead in their thirties and forties when they were looking after us.

Some people appear to thrive after trauma. Loss emboldens them, they form great ambitions and stride forward as if nothing, now, could hurt them. They are exhibits in those old stories about disaster being character-building, strength in adversity. My experience, to my shame, was nothing like this. I couldn't find it in me to do much more than reel from one day and year to the next, with little optimism about what lay ahead. I must have been difficult to be around: self-destructive, and full of anger and denial. Friendships and romances were made and then unraveled. I got wrecked as often as I could, and stayed up late watching westerns and film noir. I daydreamed about staying in bed for weeks at a time, ignoring the phone and letting everything slide.

None of this I recognized as grief. I called it being fucked up, being stressed out, a proportionate response to difficult circumstances, and, only much later, depression. I had no idea how to grieve. I watched others openly mourn the loss of friends, pets, family members. Even now, I still read op-eds by writers with something coherent to say about their mother's recent death, and I have no idea how they do it. I was angrily envious of friends who'd followed a careless path through their twenties, who'd been free to fight with their parents, to abandon their jobs or degrees and take up new ones, to take risks, to follow their silly schoolgirl dreams, to screw up and be bailed out, to know where they were in the world.

*

I somehow managed to finish my honors thesis the year after Mum and Dad died and, after ingloriously dropping out of law school, enrolled in a PhD program in literature. The discipline and order of that long dissertation provided me with a structure, one that made it easier for me to avoid social situations in which I felt uncomfortable. If people were worried about me, most of them accepted my academic commitments as a reason to leave me alone.

I won a scholarship to study in Paris for a year, but being far from Sydney didn't make me any happier. I read Stein and Bergson, Pound and Vico, Joyce and Dante. The difficult rhythms of writing suited me, and so did the isolation. I thought I would never finish my dissertation, but I did. I taught undergrads about books and films, and when I felt under siege, I turned off my phone and read. I put a lot of effort into presenting a coherent front to the world. Mostly, though, I felt at the edge of a breakdown, terrified that I'd fall and then shatter.

I'm aware, as I write this, of how unhealthy my behavior sounds. It was, and I wish I'd gauged my sadness sooner. I wish I hadn't been so convincing a performer, that I'd been able to respond honestly to all those kind questions about my state of being. What, I wonder now, should I have done? Seen a therapist or taken antidepressants sooner? Tried to come to terms with the reality of my parents' deaths, and not just dealt with the consequences? Weekends away? Massages, meditation, laughter yoga? At any rate, I think running would have seemed too literal a response. All I wanted to do was run away from my life. I was hardly going to actualize this desire by taking up jogging: an activity for light-hearted people who brushed their hair each day and enjoyed interesting vacations, not for me.

I was the recipient of a lot of good-hearted advice, including the wise and frequent counsel, *Do some exercise.* I wasn't entirely sedentary. I commuted around Sydney by bike and occasionally went to yoga classes. I swam laps every so often. Once, I joined a gym but gave it up, horrified, after two visits. I have a half-memory of running around Enmore Park on a cold afternoon, during a particularly unhappy period. I'm not sure why I set out, just that I wore green shorts and it was a one-off. I must have hoped it would help, and it didn't.

But as time passed, life became a little steadier. When two friends ran the Sydney Marathon—in 2005, I think—I met them at the finish line by the water in the Royal Botanic Gardens. I found them sprawled on the lawn, eating bananas. We were surrounded by exhausted, elated bodies. What were they all thinking about? What would it feel like to have run that far, to have kept moving for so long? I had a vision of the mental spaciousness in which they were lolling. Although I was colossally impressed, it was hardly a conversion experience. On the way home, I chortled to myself that it would be easier for me to learn Mandarin or complete a PhD in astrophysics than to run a marathon. My father had never run one, but he'd loved multisport endurance events. As a teenager, that unnecessary exertion had struck me as outlandish. When Dad strode into the house after a run, his "Albury Road Runners" T-shirt stinky, cracking jokes and laughing at them, I'd scoffed. Now I was a little curious, and I paid attention whenever marathons were mentioned. Marathons! *Imagine running a marathon!* The idea stayed with me, and I kept adding to my mental list of difficult things that would be easier than running 26 miles, such as stopping smoking, sorting my life out, or filing all the legal correspondence that was stacked in boxes under my desk.

*

I submitted my PhD in 2005 and finally graduated in 2006. My sisters had built lives for themselves by then. I had long dreamed of careless travel, and in 2007, I bought a one-way ticket to Bangkok with a view to roaming for as long as I could. My plan-that-wasn't-a-plan was to cover as much distance as possible, preferably without leaving the ground.

I took the night train to Chiang Mai from Bangkok, the slow train to Mombasa from Nairobi, the Eurostar to Paris from London. I tried to reach a museum devoted to Andy Warhol in eastern Slovenia, but couldn't figure out the bus timetable and drank beer in the town square instead. I caught the bus to Vang Vieng from Vientiane and then all the way to Luang Prabang, to Chisinau from Odessa, to Varanasi from Patna. On the ferry to Bastia from Marseilles, I slept on the floor and remembered that sad night on the doorstep.

Mostly I was alone, knotting a string of variations on the themes of repetition, movement, and forgetting. I picked a path through the broken sidewalks of Bucharest; I climbed to the top of a Corsican mountain and traipsed back down the other side. My mind dislodged as I watched scorpions fight and overripe mangos fall into the dirt during a meditation retreat in the hills behind Mandalay. (The damage done to my hips from sitting cross-legged on a wooden floor for two weeks still returns as pain in cold weather.) In corrugated-iron and bamboo

sheds jerry-rigged with wires for ancient modems and comput-
ers, I waited for Skype to load so that I could speak to my family. I told lies about my life, that my parents didn't mind me
traveling on my own, that I'd be meeting my jealous husband
at the next port, that I'd be waiting in a particular cafe the day
after tomorrow.

A year after I'd left Sydney, I sat with my family in the
front seats of a bus driving through Rajasthan. By now, the
steel frame of the hiking pack my father had chosen for my
nineteenth birthday had worked through the canvas and was a
hazard to handlers. The bus passenger list reflected the shifting
calibrations of a family life: my aunt Anne; two sisters, Lucy
and Laura; two cousins, Ali and Laurie; and Anna, Ali's girl-
friend, now wife. Claudia was at home with her husband, looking after their three kids.

The company was a delight. We took the high desert road between the dream city of Jaisalmer and the enormous colonnaded
fort at Bikaner. We played long games of cricket at roadside
stops with the mountains behind us. Our talk somehow turned
to marathons. In the vastness of northern India, where time and
space and habit seemed to me so distorted, and after all those
buses and trains, talk of these dimensions didn't feel so incongruous. Unlike me, my cousins are superb athletes, exactly the
type of people you'd expect to run marathons. Courting impos-
sibility, I joined in, declaring that one day I too would run one.

Running—of course! I'd been preoccupied with distance
and endurance and bloody running away for years. I was
caught by a weird sense of mission: I would work out how to
run for long enough that being still would be a consolation. I'd
sat on buses for so many days that I'd forgotten the city I'd left,

for so long that I'd lost sight of my destination. I wanted to take my body into the landscape and run into the world, to move with its rhythms, and to forget where I was going. I would run a marathon. "That doesn't sound like you," they said. (They were right, it was utterly out of character.) "Well, it is," I replied. *I bet you can't. I bet I can.*

*

A few months later I flew back to Sydney and started running on a treadmill. To my surprise, it didn't feel like punishment at all. After that long overture, I can't really recollect any vivid scene of beginning. I must have climbed the orange-carpeted stairs to the gym and inquired about a preliminary membership arrangement. I have no great defining memory of the moment I first stepped on a treadmill. I would have looked at those flickering controls, gingerly pressed a few buttons and started to run—very slowly.

I had conjured up some big ideas about running but had no firm idea about how I'd become a runner. My sense of myself as a fledgling athlete had many limits, the most notable being that I didn't want to run outside. The treadmill was far less daunting to me than the idea of running in public. Sydney's parks are full of fit, athletic joggers, and the awkward schoolgirl in me suspected that these gazelle-like beings might laugh at me or accidentally push me over as they zoomed past. I also worried about slipping on wet leaves and spraining my ankle, or tripping on a broken piece of pavement and tearing my knees open. I worried that I'd get lost and run out of juice, like a sick toy, and not be able to get home. I worried about blisters, sports bras, dehydration, and where to put my keys. I worried about running in the dark and being chased into the trees, and I worried about my face getting sunburned. I worried about bumping into someone I knew, scarlet-faced and puffing, and having to laugh with them about how ridiculous I looked.

Had I started in the park, not one jot of attention would have been directed my way. Now when I see novice runners out of breath on the hills, my former faint-heartedness seems histrionic. Even so, if I hadn't started running on a treadmill, I might not have started at all. It was precisely the anonymity and impersonality of the gym that kept me going. I liked feeling that I was nowhere and no one: a person with no past, in a place that could be anywhere. I stepped off the street and into an artificial reality where life was measured in minutes and calories, pounds and miles.

I felt unusually inconspicuous in the gym I'd chosen to join. It was located next to a strip club and it had very few patrons, which is also why it shut down years ago. The imaginary gyms that cause me so much disquiet are slick and corporate: this one was reassuringly grotty, reeking of stale sweat and buckets of disinfectant. The large, sunny weight room was frequented by off-duty security guards and local tough guys who ignored me. The treadmills were hidden up on a mezzanine level; most of the time, I slogged away on my own. I never joined an exercise class and generally avoided eye contact with other patrons. The winking red lights on the treadmill dashboard were mesmerizing, and I listened to podcasts to drown out any noises (daytime soaps, cruising musclemen, couples on the cardio machines), keeping my eyes on the control panel as miles and hours accrued.

There I was, running on a treadmill, squashed into an exercise cubicle like a robot athlete—and yet I felt wildly alive. What a glorious paradox. I was used to the sensory world yielding pain and fatigue. Now I was aware of my limbs and my lungs, of the sweat dripping down my neck and the thudding rhythm of my feet. My chest carried my body forward, my weight pitched through the concertina of bones at the front of my foot, my hips surprisingly still. It was only as I walked home, ruddy and merry, that I returned to my usual state of anxious self-consciousness. I was sharing an apartment with Laura, and she bore my excited babble about this beginning with great patience.

The gym offered a discount on personal training. For a month or so, I met each week with a woman called Lisa who taught me a series of stretches and insisted on calling the City2Surf my "training goal." She had a lot to say about crunches and quad strength and the importance of my core. She was very kind and a bit dorky, and her advice was helpful. I couldn't fit her into my almanac of gym idiots.

A detailed account of a person getting fitter is always tedious. What happened is that I kept running on the treadmill and found that I could run farther and farther. I began to stretch a little behind the treadmills after each run, enjoying my new proficiency in tension and release. Not every session was uplifting, but the cumulative effect was. I tracked my progress on a piece of paper shoved into my diary, and I marveled at the improvements. No science to it: I just pushed the speed arrows a little faster and stayed on the machine a little longer each time. I bounced home when I was able to run 5 miles at a stretch and shouted about it to Laura.

I've heard people say that they launched into a running program on the back of a New Year's resolution, and that their body hated them for it. Not me. I slept soundly. I took a new interest in my body, in the big muscles at the tops of my legs, in the position of my shoulders relative to my hips. Those notorious endorphin drafts shot through my limbs if I ran for long enough. This, finally, was what it was like to live in a body, to thrill in movement.

*

I'd been keeping my new habit quiet. I thought my peers would be as shocked as I was to discover not just that I enjoyed running, but also that I was planning to run the City2Surf. In this, I was mistaken. The responses were low-key. A few raised eyebrows, perhaps, but otherwise my enthusiasm was greeted with patience and support. I kept at it, pushing the speed arrows, watching the distance log, and when I'd run 14 kilometers on the treadmill, I entered the race. By the time I lined up to start the City2Surf, that rolling loop at the gym was the only surface on which I'd run.

On the day of the race, I arrived far too early and shivered for an hour as I waited for the action, telling myself to impersonate a runner so I'd fit into the crowd. Even though I had friends in the pack, I'd opted to run alone. As if I wanted to join a community of runners: I'd done everything I could to make my running a solo, even covert, endeavor. That me-versus-the-world narrative was shattered when I found myself in a crowd of seventy thousand people.

The starting gun was fired, and I began to run. No one

laughed at me. I was perfectly prepared—overprepared, actually. I swerved away from sprinklers at Rushcutters Bay, and waved at the old men playing trumpets and banjos in Dover Heights. The big hill that I'd been warned about, Heartbreak Hill, was nothing like the edifice I'd been dreading. I didn't have to convince myself to keep going, I just remembered how far I'd already come and let my feet take me all the way to the beach. The morning turned into one of those cold, sunny winter days that cast such a spectacular light on the water, and I reached Bondi with a smile on my face. That's when I discovered that the painful thing about the City2Surf isn't running it, but getting home afterward.

As it happens, the things that get said to the grieving aren't that different from the consolations offered to runners: *Just keep going. It will all be over soon. You'll get there.* Would I have started running if I hadn't been exhausted by grief—or, rather, by avoiding it? Certainly I was well practiced in denying discomfort, in plodding along and watching the clock tick. It might have made less sense to step onto a treadmill if I hadn't spent ten years feeling that I'd done nothing but flail, getting nowhere. It's reassuring to think that all the difficulties before I started running somehow primed me for what followed.

That would make for a neat story. The truth is, mine isn't really a tale of redemption through running. The world had begun to move around me before I stretched out my legs, and I had begun to travel around the world. Already, I was cautiously emerging from that long retreat. What I wasn't prepared for, though, was the sheer pleasure of movement, the extraordinary effect of that shift in attention to my legs, my breath, my pulse. After a long wait, it felt as though I might be going somewhere.

3

BORN TO RUN

One version of the story about the first woman to run a marathon goes like this: it's 1896, March, the month before the first modern Olympics took place. A Greek woman wants to compete in the marathon, the most anticipated event on the program. She runs from the town of Marathon to Athens in four and a half hours to prove that she can do it, a gutsy effort. No, say the organizers, women did not run in the ancient games, nor shall they run in ours. In the name of historical accuracy, the woman is sent home.

The woman who ran from Marathon to Athens took "Melpomene" as her pseudonym, after one of the nine muse-daughters of Zeus and Mnemosyne. It's a name derived from the Greek verb that means "to celebrate with dance or song." The mythological Melpomene was first named the muse of singing, then that of tragedy. This origin of the woman runner's chosen name lends her story a mythic sheen, which also diverts attention from the fact that it's pretty short on detail. Why did this woman choose the muse of tragedy as her classical alter ego and not, say, Athena Nike, the goddess of victory, or Artemis the hunter? Maybe this pseudonym was a sign that "Melpomene" had a dry sense of humor.

In one variation of the story, the race officials forgot her name and instead called her Melpomene, because, in historian Ana Miragaya's words, "they could see only tragedy, not her extraordinary feat." What did they view as tragic—the spectacle of a woman running such a long way, or the likelihood that her achievement would be forgotten?

One of the few published accounts of her run appeared in a French-language newspaper in Greece, *Le Messager d'Athènes*. That brief report contains one vivid detail: Melpomene stopped only once, halfway through, and only for ten minutes, to eat oranges. "*Sucer quelques oranges*" is how the journalist puts it: "to suck down a few oranges." We know so little about Melpomene, but this detail helps us fathom her thirst and, as we picture the juice running down her neck, we may suppose that she was a woman who didn't squander time on unnecessarily long breaks. I often crave sugary citrus when I run for a long time: my thoughts turn to lemon gelato, sticky orange cordial, margaritas, salty-sweet energy drinks, and fat, juicy oranges like Melpomene's.

There's another story in circulation about a woman and that first marathon: this one involves a thirty-year-old single mother named Stamata Revithi, who was traveling from her home in Piraeus to Athens to look for work. One of her children had just died, and she needed money to feed the child who had survived. She met a man who advised her to seek renown by running in the Olympic marathon—so she changed direction and walked to Marathon.

Why not? She must have thought it over as she walked, because when the international journalists at Marathon asked her why she was planning to enter, she had an answer ready: "So that the King might give my child a position in the future." She reckoned it would take her three and a half hours, adding, "It may be even less. I saw in a dream that I had an apron full of gold and gilded sugared almonds! Who knows! My heart is in it, I suppose my feet will hold." Children and money are rarely plot points in the big stories that get told about running, though for many women who run, they're important considerations. Who can afford the time to run? And who will look after the kids?

Stamata Revithi's readiness to undertake a tremendous physical feat to help her kid sounds as if it's made for daytime television. In fact, *See How She Runs*, a 1978 made-for-TV movie starring Joanne Woodward, follows a pretty similar storyline: a newly single mother gets her life together and regains the respect of her kids as she trains for the Boston Marathon. The calm rhythms of running help her resolve the chaos in her personal life. It's one of the few books or films I've encountered that depicts a woman runner in an unambiguously positive light. The difference is in the ending. Woodward's character aces her race; Revithi wasn't allowed to enter the 1896 Olympic marathon—instead, she completed the course the day after the official event in five and a half long hours.

I wonder what this runner who tried to get a start looked like. No one took a photo of her. Did she have a classic runner's physique: not too tall, long limbs, slim shoulders and hips? Did the journalists talk among themselves about whether she was too thin, or too tall, or a little heavy in the thighs? How much of her body would she have been expected to cover?

Historians have sparred over whether Melpomene and Revithi were the same woman. Most of the official male entrants who started the 1896 marathon dropped out en route, but in both these half-told tales, the women go the distance—even though neither was allowed to enter the new Panathinaiko Stadium for a final lap and had to run around it to finish. On March 29, 1896, a young Greek man of humble birth named Spyridon Louis won the first marathon ever run in just under three hours. He became a national hero. There's no record of what happened to Revithi—or to Melpomene. Neither woman is granted more than an apologetic footnote in commentary on that first marathon.

*

It's plausible that neither of my grandmothers would ever have run more than a mile at a stretch in her life. Their mothers, who would have been girls when Victoria sat on the throne of England, were even less likely to have done so. Some runners might be able to trace an athletic lineage and say to themselves, *This love of running came from my grandmother; I was born to run long distances.* There are no Melpomenes in my family tree. In fact, I don't recall even once seeing my father's mother, Nana, wearing trousers or shorts. She wore skirts and uncreased shirts with silver brooches; her white hair was always precisely tucked behind her ears. A brilliant, impatient woman, she left the workforce when the first of her seven children was born and never went back. Her children and grandchildren were expected to plow tirelessly the opportunities she hadn't been given. "Once you've made up your mind," she advised me, "never, ever change it." I didn't inherit her adamantine demeanor; had I, I would have become a tougher runner, less inclined to slow down and walk, more determined to keep going. I doubt Nana ever considered running a marathon, but had she decided to do so when she was in her thirties, even she would have been turned back at the starting line.

My mother's mother, Grandma, thought of herself as more modern, and she did wear trousers, though she called them slacks and matched them with strappy sandals and painted toenails. I know that she played tennis with my grandfather when my mother was growing up, but it is impossible for me to imagine her wearing either sneakers or shorts. Jeans were sloppy, she thought, and she often cautioned me against wearing trainers when I was a student. My feet would become too accustomed to comfortable shoes, she said, and I'd never be able to wear heels. For Grandma, the only thing worse than a visible bra strap was no bra at all. Girls should never gobble their meals lest they be thought greedy. Horses sweat, men perspire, women glow: the messiness of running, the rank physicality of it all, would have bothered her, I think. She died before I started running, and by then she'd stopped worrying so much about my unbrushed hair and my pierced nose. Had she lived to hear me get excited about running, I might have found that she had changed her views.

Both my grandmothers were born in 1914 and were city teenagers in the hungry 1930s. Did they run around playgrounds and parks when they were young, and if so, when did they stop? In the 1930s, women were encouraged to foster their health and beauty through physical culture. Swimming, calisthenics, cycling and dancing were sanctioned activities, but strenuous exertion was discouraged as it was thought to imperil fertility. Any undertaking can be dangerous at extremes—however, the risks of vigorous exercise for women, including running long distances, were by today's reckonings wildly overstated.

By the 1940s, the world was at war and my grandmothers' husbands had enlisted. Grandma worked in advertising and sang in a radio trio with her sisters; Nana looked after her eldest children. I can no more picture them running than I can see them roller-skating or hitchhiking or chewing gum, though it's not impossible, I suppose, that they did all these things.

When my parents were kids, the photo albums tell stories of suburban Australian home life: beaches, gardens, carefully posed group portraits. Times would have changed enough for my mother and aunts to have been herded into school cross-country events. My aunt Anne is a fine runner, and I've completed many races with her and her children. I don't think my mother was an enthusiastic school athlete, and she certainly wasn't a runner. She liked to kayak on the Murray River in summer and to cross-country ski in winter. If I ever saw her playing a team sport as an adult, that memory has gone. If she'd lived, maybe we would have spoken about the remarkable generational shifts in thinking about women's bodies that we'd both witnessed.

Strict grandmothers who believe in dress codes and good manners don't usually feature in stories about long-distance running—but they should. For the greater part of the twentieth century, women who ran anything like what we now think of as long distances were chided as if they were naughty girls. Modest women would not sanction visibly moving breasts. Sweat was grotesque, unfeminine, unattractive. Renegade women who did want to run were warned of dire physical consequences. It was thought that running might generate abnormal hungers and thirsts. And what other freedoms would wayward women athletes demand? If women couldn't control their own bodies, rigid social norms would.

*

I first stumbled across a reference to Melpomene on a website devoted to women's running. It was an appealingly improbable story, one that also signaled to me how little I knew about the history of women's distance running. I thought that to remedy this I'd just need to visit a library and borrow a book about women's athletics. It turns out that very few such books have been written. Before the 1960s, only a handful of female long-distance runners are on record—and their stories have been as patchily recorded as Melpomene's. These women intrigued me; running wasn't an activity I'd ever associated with insubordination. As is the case with disruptive women today, crowds of mockers belittled their achievements, while persons of influence called for their outrageous conduct to cease.

Where to begin? I was looking for predecessors. I wanted to grasp whom I was following when I lined up to start a race. I soon learned that tough-as-nails women competed in the brutal pedestrian races of the nineteenth century in England, the United States, and Australia. Peter Radford—one of the few historians who has rummaged extensively in the archives of women's sports—has gathered accounts of an extraordinary variety of women who ran for money on the pedestrian circuit, including a seventy-year-old Scottish woman who attempted to run 96 miles in twenty-four hours in 1833 (and was arrested for causing a public disturbance), and an eight-year-old who raced in several 30- and 40-mile events in 1823. Radford adds, as if making an aside to one of my grandmothers over drinks, "there were not, however, as far as we know any ladies."

In the United States, women pedestrian runners issued audacious challenges to male champions, while spectators were invited to bet on the outcomes. It sounds like a rough scene, and all the runners were professionals, not amateurs. I'm tempted to draw a line between the brutal pedestrian races and go-hard-or-go-home boot-camp regimens, but the match is hardly exact. Women pedestrians were catcalled, harassed, ogled, and pelted with stones as they ran. What they had in common was that they ran for money: a blithe love of movement had nothing to do with it, nor did a desire to harden up or prove a point.

Not all cultures have bristled at the idea of women running. There's evidence, for example, that running long distances was part of girls' initiation rituals in some Native American nations. The Tarahumara people ran between their villages in the hills of northern Mexico as a matter of course. Nina Kuscsik, who argued the case for a women's Olympic marathon in the 1970s, borrows a story from a *Sports Illustrated* article by Edwin Shrake that shows that the women who ran in those villages were not viewed as first-class runners: "in the 1920s an emissary went to a Tarahumara chief to invite him to send runners to a marathon race in Kansas. When told that a marathon was a mere 26 miles, the chief ordered three girls to run it." The chief might have viewed women as second-class runners—but he knew they wouldn't have trouble with a marathon.

Native American women and men both participated in the pedestrian events of the late nineteenth century and, when they did, much was made of their racial identities. Australian Indigenous men, including the legendary Charlie Samuels, were also prominent figures on the international pedestrian circuit, but I've encountered no records of Australian Indigenous women who gained renown through running. What did the figure of the woman runner mean in Australian Indigenous cultures—and how, I wonder, did settlement shift that meaning? If Indigenous women once ran for pleasure or to hunt, I fear that many would later have had cause to run in terror. Gaps in the record and inattentive historians have thwarted my efforts to piece together any kind of narrative of women's bodies in motion; information about those women whose lives have until recently stayed on the margins of history, especially working-class women and Indigenous women, has been even more sparse.

In Europe, very occasionally, the cause of public entertainment was served by women runners. One such event, La Marche des Midinettes, run on a 7.5-mile course from Paris to Nanterre, first took place in 1903. The midinettes were women who worked in fashion: shop assistants, seamstresses, models. Twenty-five hundred of them reportedly competed in the first Marche; tens of thousands of spectators cheered as they set off from the Place de la Concorde. This event is much more recognizable to me than the pedestrian races. Although it lacked corporate sponsorship, it sounds like an early predecessor to She Runs the Night, a fun night out rather than a serious competition—at least, that's the impression I formed from photographs and illustrations. Unfortunately, the attending journalists didn't ask the midinettes about why they were running or how they'd trained. Instead, drooling commentary on the pleasures of watching young women run went to press the following week.

There's always been an audience keen to gawk at women athletes with their corsets loosened. This goes some way to explain the cautious approach taken to organized women's athletics. For example, the first-ever women's collegiate field day, held at Vassar College in the United States in 1895, was conducted under extremely modest conditions: participants were shielded by trees, with no men present save the referee, a presumably chaste-minded professor of classics. The athletics program included 100-yard and 220-yard dashes.

In 1922, the U.S. Amateur Athletic Union decided that 220 yards (200 meters) would be the longest distance women athletes could run in that country. Over the next decade, a few troublemaking dissenters organized women's athletics events that included longer runs. One of these rebels, a Frenchwoman named Alice Milliat, helped to convince the International Olympic Committee to add athletic events for women to its program. She later recalled, "those first sportswomen who dared to brave public opinion and to bring shame on their families were viewed as wild, emotionally disturbed, fanatic women using sport only as an occasion for a brawl."

After much disputation and public concern, an agreement was reached to conduct five women's athletics events at the 1928 Olympics in Amsterdam—including an 800-meter race.

That historic race was, alas, a disaster for women's long-distance running. Three of the runners bettered the previous world record, but three others collapsed at the finish line. These swooning women seemed to confirm what many observers had suspected—long-distance runs were bad for women. The International Athletics Federation was lobbied by sports organizations and sundry guardians of the public good to cancel women's distance events. Women didn't race the 800 meters at the Olympic level again until 1960.

*

A few rare birds in the first half of the twentieth century set themselves to running extremely long distances. Take the first woman to finish South Africa's Comrades Marathon, a race that's actually much longer than a marathon—it's a hard-ass 55 miles between Pietermaritzburg and Durban. Neither women nor nonwhite athletes were allowed to compete as official entrants until 1975. The event is still being run today, and when two of my cousins entered a few years ago, I followed their progress online in real time, horrified both by the hills they scaled and by the distance they covered.

Somehow, Frances Hayward, a white typist from a Durban bank, was allowed to run the race in 1923. She finished 28th, but couldn't be awarded a Comrades medal as she wasn't an official entrant, so spectators and other runners chipped in and collected money to buy her a tea service and a rose bowl.

I would love to have interviewed her. What did she do with the tea service—smash it? How did she get fit enough to run 55 miles, and did she train alone? I'd also ask her the same question I ask everyone I meet who has entered one of these ultramarathons: What the hell made you want to do this? In the absence of answers to these questions, the striking aspects of Hayward's story are that she had a will to enter the race, was strong enough to finish it, and wasn't bodily prevented by officials from starting.

The woman with the strongest claim to be celebrated as the first dedicated amateur distance runner was Violet Piercy. In 1926, when she was about thirty-seven, she ran the Polytechnic marathon course from Windsor Castle to Stamford Bridge in three hours and forty minutes. A timed run, not a race. There's no way a woman would have been allowed to enter a marathon as an official competitor in 1926.

Journalists were incredulous that a woman could run the marathon distance—and do so in less than four hours. Tired of the questions, Piercy made her point by running long distances again and again. In 1927, she broke what she claimed was her own record for a 10-mile run (not that there were other women lining up to contest 10-milers). In 1928, she had another go at a timed marathon, but retired 6 miles from the finish line due to hot weather. In 1933, she ran the marathon distance twice—both times in heavy rain. Because she'd never run a marathon under race conditions, doubts persisted. Finally, in 1936, with what the *Oxford Dictionary of National Biography* calls the "connivance" of the organizers of the Polytechnic Harriers race, Piercy ran alongside the men and finished in four and a half hours.

She must have had immense confidence in her capacities to set off on any of her runs. What was the source of her self-assurance? No one just leaps out of bed in the morning and runs a marathon—it takes reserves of physical fitness and months of training. Piercy was a member of the Mitcham Athletic Club, but there was absolutely no culture of women's distance running to support her. Did she train by pounding out hundreds of laps?

In 1927 Piercy agreed to be filmed for a wonderfully rich silent Pathé newsreel titled *The Runner*. The opening slide reads, "Anyone here like to run 26½ miles non-stop . . . ? This lady did . . . from London to Windsor, in record time (for a lady) . . ." We see her running with male chaperones on bicycles. They're all trailed by another man driving a car. Was this kind of supervisory entourage de rigueur for all women athletes? How irksome that must have been. How could Piercy possibly have organized regular runs under such conditions? The newsreel is staged, but it makes me all the more curious about what it was like to run as a woman when no others were doing so. It's possible that some annoying schoolboy told Piercy she'd never be much of a runner—because she was a woman—and then she set herself to proving him wrong.

Violet Piercy is hardly well known. As a dedicated female distance runner, she has no precedents except the professional pedestrians, and it seems she left no legacy. When the *Dictionary of National Biography* was compiling her entry, the editors made inquiries about her identity to a group of British sports historians. The birthdates of five possible Violet Piercys were put forward. A brief article in a 2009 *Track Stats* magazine sniffily notes:

we are still no further forward in establishing for certain the validity of Miss Piercy's pioneering effort. What we do know is that it was achieved in off circumstances, as were other of her distance-running enterprises, and that she was evidently a skilled seeker after self-publicity.

"Off circumstances" sounds a bit disreputable. That Piercy sought publicity, spoke to journalists, and recorded a news-reel are the reasons we know more about her than about Melpomene.

The International Association of Athletics Federations (IAAF) credits Piercy with the first women's world's best marathon time for her 1926 Polytechnic run. However, there are a number of accreditation bodies for such records, and they don't always agree. Bickering over the technicalities has overwhelmed an astonishing proportion of women's marathon records, so the instability of Piercy's status is typical. Here's the gist of it: the IAAF has only recognized marathon world records as such since 2004. Before that, the variability of courses meant that it only kept track of "world's best times." Because Piercy didn't complete her marathon under official race conditions, some historians argue that it shouldn't be recognized. If we choose to take her time at face value, and agree that the difference between "world's best" and "world records" is semantic, hers is the longest-standing record in the history of athletics. An extraordinary achievement. Her record wasn't broken until 1963, when a young American, Merry Lepper, ran the Western Hemisphere Marathon in Culver City, California, in 3:37:07.

An alternative accreditation body, the Association of Road

Running Statisticians, lists an earlier world's best women's marathon time: a Frenchwoman named Marie-Louise Ledru, according to the association's books, ran the Tour de Paris Marathon in September 1918 in five hours and forty minutes. This isn't a fast marathon—Ledru must have walked for long stretches. Her time is a rare world's best, in that it's one that most moderately fit, moderately trained marathon runners would be able to surpass. But where was a woman to turn for marathon training advice in 1918?

There's even less on the record about Ledru than about Piercy—who she was or why she decided to run a marathon just before the end of a bloody war. What does exist is her photograph, taken at the starting line. A bib printed with "171" is pinned to her loose dress, which has a broad white collar tied into a black bow. Her skirt falls to her ankles over a pair of tightly laced black boots. She's the odd one out in a crowd of men wearing shorts, jerseys, and simple light shoes. The mood is quite different to that of Le Marche des Midinettes: no one is smiling. Ledru stares straight at the camera, her hands behind her back and her hips jutting forward. Something about her demeanor strikes me as defiant, as if she'd had to argue with the photographer or a race official to pose with the men. Was that her only long run, or did she jostle her way to the start of other marathons, as Piercy did? We simply don't know.

*

If I'm looking to grasp some genealogical connection to a running past, it's because the shared history of women's running is full of discontinuities and exceptions—and it's largely bound by the start and finish lines of races, by the records of who ran first and who ran fastest. I was born the granddaughter of two women who wouldn't, I think, have seen anything amiss about restrictions on the distances women might run. Both those grandmothers are dead and I can't ask them whether the idea of running a marathon ever grabbed them. Probably not—and my best guess is that neither of them knew of Violet Piercy. I can't ask my mother whether the women's 800-meter race at the 1960 Olympics meant anything to her, or whether *she* ever thought about running a marathon. Again, probably not—but she would have been well qualified to scrutinize medical evidence about the effects of distance running on women's bodies.

Even with imagination and guesswork, I've found it difficult to answer the questions that really move me. Who were these women, and why did they run? Should I hail them as heroes? What else did they stand for in their lives? They appear to me as the faintest of sketches. What sense is there to make out of Melpomene's oranges, Stamatha Revithi's dream of sugared almonds, Frances Hayward's tea set, Violet Piercy's chaperones, and Marie-Louise Ledru's weary glare?

There are surely other names, lost in dusty sports archives and municipal records, that I didn't find. And then there are the brilliant athletes who might have wanted to run and weren't allowed to, whether by sports officials, their mothers, or their husbands. I wish I knew who they were and why they ran. Nobody remembers. It's incredible to me that nobody bothered to ask.

4

RUNNING LIKE A GIRL

If you call yourself a runner, people suppose that you have some innate athletic capacity that you've cannily kept hidden. In my case, this simply isn't true. I was not cast from the same mold as the female running pioneers. There's no false modesty here—I'm woefully uncoordinated. I never had my hopes of competing with the school cross-country team dashed, because I never would have wished such a burden on myself. I wasn't chosen last for school sports teams because I was wildly unpopular: I was left waiting because I was a dead loss on the field.

Each of us has a gruesome story to tell about our adolescent body. The theme of mine is a failure of proprioception, an inability to control my limbs. Athleticism, the fluent realization of coordination, muscularity, skill, reflexes, and, above all, will, was beyond me. For me, as for many other awkward, uncoordinated kids, school sports were an intense and frequent humiliation. I was teased about this, of course, although not with any extraordinary viciousness; what I hated was that my athletic failures couldn't be hidden. The kids who botched their algebra quizzes didn't have their mistakes paraded in front of the class. Every catch I dropped, I dropped before an audience. That's how I remember it, anyway.

When I graduated from high school, the headmaster wrote me a reference with a backhanded plaudit about my persistence: "Not a natural athlete, Catriona always tries her best on the sporting field." Mostly, I did try very hard. Mortified by my lack of coordination, I willed myself to catch the softball as I traced its downward arc. My hands were always in the wrong place and the ball always bounced to a thud on the grass. My parents were firm believers in the virtues of netball, hockey, and tennis, and so for years I double-faulted, fumbled catches, tripped over my shoelaces, and generally let the team down. Even though I rarely managed to return serve, my mother was adamant that playing tennis would be a useful social skill when I grew up. Were these ordeals supposed to inculcate some kind of resilience in me? I'll never know. If my parents hoped that my coordination would improve through practice, they would have been disappointed. I still can't catch and I don't play tennis.

Most of all, though, I hated running. Laps around the school grounds were assigned to pupils as punishment for leaving our maroon and sickly blue gym clothes at home. I could think of no crueler consequence for forgetfulness. Running left my cheeks in flames and made me gasp. In my last two years of high school, I counted it a major victory that I was able to avoid consecutive cross-country meets in order to sing out of key at the local choir festival.

*

In the thirty-seven years that passed before Violet Piercy's marathon time was bested, the world went to war, my mother and father were born, the men's marathon record plummeted, athletes were anointed heroes—and no one really took seriously the proposition that a woman might want to run a marathon. When Merry Lepper finished the Western Hemisphere Marathon in 3:37:07 at Culver City in 1963, rather than being delighted by this sentimental first—*Twenty-year-old California girl breaks the world record!*—the race organizers were indignant that she'd run in the first place. Marathoners like Jim Peters, Sergei Popov, and Abebe Bikila made headlines around the world when they broke records, but almost no one noticed Lepper.

The early 1960s marks a transitional period in women's running: more women ran long distances and even more challenged received ideas about what their bodies could do. Journalists spoke with these pioneering runners and, eventually, so did historians. Some of them even wrote memoirs. And so we know that Lepper hid on the sidelines, in the bushes, as she waited for her marathon to start. Lepper's concern that she might be pulled off the course was well founded: women in the United States were forbidden from racing any distance over a mile and a half.

Unlike the women we've met so far, Lepper didn't run alone.

She trained and raced with a friend named Lyn Carman, under the guidance of Carman's husband, a marathon coach. Decades later, Carman recalled, "Before the race, there was one official who spent about 20 minutes chewing me out, saying I'd never have babies again." When another official tried to haul the two women out of the race, Carman punched him. I imagine these scenes as a sequence of comic frames: the two women concealed in shrubbery; the baby lecture; the punch.

Twenty miles in, Carman dropped out—but Lepper kept going. She told interviewers that it was Carman's grit that had inspired her to start the race. What kept her going? She couldn't bear the thought that the first two women to attempt a marathon in the United States would both fail to finish. Lepper crossed the finish line and somehow, her time—as recorded by a sympathetic official—was accepted. Although she made the front pages of local newspapers, it took a long time for her achievement to be celebrated.

Because Lepper broke a long-standing record, she's sometimes hailed as America's first female marathoner, but this isn't quite true. In 1959, Arlene Pieper finished the Pikes Peak Marathon in Colorado and managed to escape a scolding. Her nine-hour time in that very strenuous race doesn't come close to threatening Piercy's record, but she's notable for completing the 13-mile ascent of the peak with her nine-year-old daughter in tow, then leaving the girl behind so she could run the descent. Pieper is now acknowledged as the first woman to finish an American marathon as an official entrant, although no one realized it at the time.

Running historians had no contact with her at all, until in

2009, half a century after her run, the Pikes Peak organizers hired a private investigator to find her. Pieper ran a fitness studio for women in 1959, and she'd entered the marathon to promote her business. She told *Runner's World* in 2013, "I wanted to run the Boston Marathon, but they wouldn't let me. We were just supposed to stay home, bake cookies, and have babies." Until recently she was part of the shadow history of women's running, one of the little-known women whose achievements were simply forgotten. I wonder how many other stories like hers have been lost.

Meanwhile, Merry Lepper's record didn't last long. It was toppled by Scottish runner Dale Greig, on the Isle of Wight, in May 1964. Familiar themes are sounded in Greig's story: she was an experienced runner, one of the founders of the Scottish women's cross-country association—and yet she was only allowed to run her marathon on the condition that an ambulance trail her for the entire race. What a condescending stipulation, and how annoying it must have been. When her record was announced, the organizers of the event, Ryde Harriers, were reprimanded by the British Women's Amateur Athletic Association for letting her run at all.

The women's world's best actually fell twice in 1964. Here's how the second world-beating marathon of that year was reported in *Sports Illustrated*:

> One Saturday last August, a Mrs. Millie Sampson, a 31-year-old mother of two who lived in the Auckland suburb of Manurewa, went dancing until 1 am. The next day she cooked dinner for 11 visitors. In between, she ran the marathon in 3:19:33.

Actually, Sampson wasn't married and she had no children. That she knocked eight minutes off Greig's record passed without comment. Most of the article was devoted to the New Zealand middle-distance runner Peter Snell and his preparations for the upcoming world championships.

*

The successes of Piercy, Lepper, Greig, and Sampson demonstrated that at least some women could run marathons. As more women snuck into races and reached finish lines, the question of whether women should be allowed to run long distances became a topic of much wider debate. The consensus among sports officials was that they certainly should not.

In 1966, a slight woman named Roberta Gibb Bingay crouched in the bushes near the starting line of the Boston Marathon, waiting for the race to begin. She was a tremendous runner, extremely confident, and very well trained. She planned to pass herself off as a male athlete, wearing a blue hooded sweatshirt and a pair of running shoes. Women's running shoes weren't in production then, and Bingay—who has entered running history under the name Bobbi Gibb—had trained in shoes habitually worn by nurses as they paced hospital corridors.

Despite Gibb's efforts to run in drag, the spectators weren't fooled. She recalls: "as soon as the crowds saw I was a woman there was a great commotion. People called out to me wishing me good luck." Her mother later assured the *New York Times*, "Roberta doesn't want to break any barriers." A typical worried mother's effort to keep the peace, the kind of thing I can imagine my own mother saying about my early feminist engagement: *It's just a phase she's going through.* It wasn't strictly true that Gibb was running just for the hell of it: as she ran, she laughed to herself about the "preconceived prejudices [that] would crumble when I trotted right along for 26 miles." Spotted by journalists, by the time she crossed the finish line she was big news.

The Boston Marathon organizers were furious. They'd already knocked back Gibb's request for an official spot on the grounds that women weren't physiologically capable of running such distances. It was for her own good. The co–race director, Will Cloney, was widely quoted in the newspapers the next day as saying that while Gibb had run along the marathon course, she hadn't run *in* the Boston Marathon—she'd merely covered the same route as the official race while it was in progress. Of all the rhetorical contortions used to discourage women from running, this ungracious remark merits special mention.

Gibb's marathon was a minor media sensation, but when Kathrine Switzer finished the same race a year later, she hit the big time. The Syracuse University student entered the 1967 Boston Marathon by marking her name as "K. Switzer," letting the assumption that she was a man serve as her cover. She'd already chucked convention by training with the Syracuse track team. Her coach, a marathon veteran named Arnie Briggs, geared her up to run the distance. He also ran the Boston Marathon by her side, as did her boyfriend, a college athlete whose forte, helpfully, was the hammer throw.

Journalists cruising along the course in their press truck drew the attention of a race official, Jock Semple, to the presence of a young woman in the race. He leapt into the crowd of runners and tried to drag Switzer to the sidelines. She describes this intervention:

> A big man, a huge man, with bared teeth was set to pounce, and before I could react he grabbed my shoulder and flung me back screaming, "Get the hell out of my race and give me those numbers!"

This sounds like the kind of assault feared by women who run alone after dark.

Switzer's two sidekicks stepped in, pulling Semple away so she could keep going. The press truck caught the whole tussle on film, and images appeared in newspapers around the world the following day. The three men appear to be fighting over Switzer; the *LA Times* captioned the image, "Chivalry prevails." Thanks to these photographs, this episode is probably the most famous in the history of the women's marathon. Almost fifty years later, it vividly conveys the values of another time, when a woman running was highly controversial, and when men were prepared to demonstrate their power over women in a hands-on fashion. In Switzer's words: "I had never felt such embarrassment and fear. I'd never been manhandled, never even spanked as a child, and the physical power and swiftness of the attack stunned me." The brute physicality of this struggle is still alarming, a reminder that women runners who came of age in the 1960s and '70s didn't just have to pull a mind-over-matter stunt to complete a marathon—they came up against real human opposition.

In the photos, Switzer strikes me as very brave and very young. Almost every time I've run in a race, whatever the distance, I've thought about giving up. For long stretches, I've berated myself for being so foolish as to enter in the first place. I remind myself that I've done it before, that plenty of other women have too. Friends send text messages. Usually there's someone waiting for me at the finish line. I wouldn't have been able to run anywhere without these layers of reassurance, let alone when I was twenty. If I'd had to duck behind the shrubbery before I started, as Bobbi Gibb and Merry Lepper did, I would have been lost. And, once I'd set out, had I been tackled by a big man, would I have had the fortitude to continue? I doubt it. Switzer did—but not without a whole lot of grinding anxiety. She describes feeling sick, humiliated, angry, and scared. "If I quit," she recalls in her memoir, "everybody would say it was a publicity stunt." As it played out, people did accuse Switzer of seeking the limelight, just as they'd accused Violet Piercy of an untoward desire for fame forty years earlier.

After running for almost four and a half hours, Switzer crossed the finish line. Will Cloney delivered a fresh set of angry quotes to the media, deploring "American girls forcing their way into something where they're neither eligible, nor wanted. All rules throughout the world bar girls from running more than a mile and a half." As this hubbub played out, Bobbi Gibb managed again to complete the race as an unofficial runner. She ran about an hour faster than Switzer did, and avoided both the press and the race officials.

Within a few days, Switzer had been tossed out of the Amateur Athletic Union (AAU) for running with men, running more than the allowed distance, fraudulently entering an AAU event, and, astonishingly, running without a chaperone. Cloney told the *New York Times*, "If that girl were my daughter,

I'd spank her." Under pressure, the Boston Marathon organizers eventually agreed to recognize Switzer's time. (They didn't
recognize Gibb's run for several more years.) The publicity had
a galvanizing effect on women distance runners, especially on
the Eastern Seaboard of the United States, and they began to
train together with events like the Boston Marathon and the
New York City Marathon in their sights. This circle of tenacious women who kept stealing into marathons and running
faster and faster times were all fantastic, ambitious athletes.
Not one of them was a recreational runner out to see if she
could make a certain distance or turn her life around. Elite
women athletes in other sports, especially tennis, were taking
a stand against inequity too. Other women were burning their
bras, leaving their husbands, dropping acid, refusing to speak
to their fathers, writing poetry, setting up refuges, plotting revolution. The women's movement was fragmenting and reform-
ing and, as all this insurrection was underway, the best women
long-distance runners in the world kept on getting faster.

*

My schoolgirl self had no intimation that she would one day run
a marathon, that she would come to love running. She schemed
to skip running events, faked injuries, fatigue, distress. By the
time I arrived at college, refusing to participate in sports was
an act of overdue defiance. Had I then been aware of any cultural injunctions against women running long distances, I
would have viewed them as a rare blessing from the patriarchy.

Physiology explains some of this resistance: I'm not built
like a runner. My wide hips and small shoulders mean that I

have a very inefficient gait. My joints are hypermobile, and I have a tiny lung capacity. Characteristics like these are what distinguish great athletes from the very determined, and they're also what would stop me being a really strong runner if I ever actually threw myself into vigorous training.

And yet, the stories that get told about the body are what help us make sense of it. Every klutzy kid has heard the advice I was given: *relax, keep your eyes on the ball, it's all in your mind*. We hear people chortling when we run, we hear someone sighing with disappointment when we stretch in the direction of a ball without any hope of catching it. What if it really *was* all in my mind? I wonder now whether some of my discomfort about my uncooperative limbs was drawn from a deeper cultural well, the one that irrigated my grandmothers' beliefs about orderly bodies and good behavior, and that made officials so angry with Kathrine Switzer and Bobbi Gibb.

Those beliefs certainly had a solid cultural foundation. In 1837, an affable Englishman named Donald Walker wrote what was effectively the first exercise manual for women, to be read by the idle daughters of the aspiring middle class. *Exercises for Ladies, calculated to preserve and improve beauty* was mainly concerned with good posture; it did, however, include a very brief, cautionary section on running and leaping. "Owing to the excessive shock which both of these exercises communicate," Walker determined, "neither of them are very congenial to women." He summoned Rousseau to his cause: "Women are not made for running: when they fly, it is that they may be caught. Running is not the only thing they do awkwardly; but it is the only thing they do without grace."

Even after years of running, on a bad day I would mutter

to myself, *This doesn't feel quite right.* If people say things like, *Just put your mind to it, relax,* when I'm trying to park in a tight spot, I'm taken back—just for a split red second—to the humiliated eternity of the maladroit teenager. When my elbow clangs against a doorframe that I thought was yards away, when a yoga teacher tells me to stop thinking and to glide my body through an impossible sequence, I get stuck again.

I used to hold firm to the belief that any feats of physical endurance were beyond my reach. If I spend too much time thinking about my body, I still fret that it might be slightly ridiculous for me to keep running long distances. I worry that I'll trip, that I'll be left behind, that my body isn't strong enough. If once I thought all this awkwardness was my lonely biological destiny, that I just wasn't born to run, now I'm not so sure.

*

During the first half-century of the women's marathon, concerns about the effect of running long distances on women's capacity to bear children ran high. A Swiss IOC official, D.F.M. Messerli, was present at the 1928 Olympics and watched the final of the 800 meters, when all those women keeled over. Seeing himself as a great advocate for female athletes, he nonetheless favored the imposition of limits in the name of sacred maternity. In 1952, he wrote a chatty paper on women in the Games, which serves as a summary of mid-century attitudes to female athleticism.

We are of the opinion, that these restrictions are all for the good, seeing that woman has a noble task in life namely to give birth to healthy children and to bring them up in the best of conditions. We must do everything in our power to improve her conditions of living, but on the other hand, we must avoid everything which can be injurious to her health and harm her as a potential mother.

When Betty Friedan called for a "drastic reshaping of the cultural image of femininity" in her 1963 book *The Feminine Mystique*, she might have been speaking to would-be runners. "Fulfillment as a woman had only one definition for American women after 1949—the housewife-mother," she wrote.

To my surprise, now and then I still get asked if I'm worried about the effect of running on my fertility. The answer to this intrusion is always, of course, no—and if I could be bothered, I might point to the thousands of women who have run long-distance events and delivered healthy babies. Women who are trying to conceive are advised not to train for marathons, although some do, and some women temporarily stop menstruating if they rapidly lose a great deal of weight. Questions about the hormonal repercussions of training have more relevance to professionals who run in an intensive fashion over long periods, especially if they begin very young. But for the rest of us, the fertility interventions are retrograde shock tactics. In 2015, Australian newspapers reported that the principal of a Melbourne Islamic school had banned girls from running because the activity might "cause" them to lose their virginity. That's an extreme case, but it's located on a spectrum of warnings to women about the physical consequences of running: *you will stop menstruating, your breasts will shrink, your body will become unfeminine.*

There is an influential essay, by feminist philosopher Iris Marion Young, titled "Throwing Like a Girl" that explores the body experience of women. When I read it as an undergrad, I didn't really reflect on how it spoke to my own gloomy experiences with sports; when I reread it as a runner, the questions Young posed struck me as vital: What is it like to experience the space of the world as a woman? How is it gendered? How are the physical differences between men and women used to explain structural inequalities between them?

Young emphasizes the "situation" of women, scrutinizing the different ways that men and women use their bodies to perform tasks, the way they throw—and run. That situation is circumscribed by "historical, cultural, social, and economic limits." If a woman throws like a girl, restricts her movements, and doesn't hurl the ball with full force, it's not necessarily that her biceps are less developed than her brother's: her experience of the world bears on the way she brings her body into motion. As her arm moves through space, history moves with it. Young writes, "for many women as they move in sport, a space surrounds us in imagination that we are not free to move beyond; the space available to our movement is a constricted space." Young acknowledges that her analysis is culturally specific—it's about cisgender women "in contemporary advanced industrial, urban, and commercial society"—and I should issue a similar disclaimer. I'm writing first from a set of experiences that mesh well with Young's essay. The kind of complex acculturation that she describes is, however, my best explanation for the anxiety that I felt for so long about running and sports, one that so many women I've spoken to share. It's much more convincing to me than a fatalistic interpretation of physiology—or the theory that I alone am a one-woman athletic disaster.

If being told that you run like a girl carries a derogatory swipe, it's also the basis for new communities of the body, as the She Runs events, in all their bright pink, commercialized splendor, demonstrate. The upbeat T-shirts declaring that the wearer "Runs Like a Girl" or "Kicks Like a Girl" or "Fights Like a Girl" are hopeful rejections of the situation Young describes. It's a very different statement to ones that Switzer and Gibb were forced to make: that they didn't run at all like girls, that they could run as well as any man could.

*

As I was thinking over how I'd formed the idea that I couldn't run, I came across a grim study. The researchers found that talented female athletes, those who competed at national and international levels at a young age, were terribly bullied about their successes at school. These were the girls who ran faster than all the other girls, who threw farther—who had, surely, spat out some of the inhibitions that I'd swallowed. They reported being ostracized by their peers and weathering nasty taunts. None of the small sample surveyed by Maureen O'Neill and Angie Calder were asked whether they'd been bullied: all the young women and none of the young men volunteered that this was the case.

Had I made fun of excellent athletes when I was at school? I remember being envious of those girls who made jumping rope, swinging bats, and running laps look easy. They weren't national athletes, but I don't recall teasing them. My ineptitude on the field made me a target of unkindness, and I didn't want any more attention. Beyond a bit of what-do-I-care-about-sports-anyway, I didn't sling anything back. It's distressing to me now to contemplate that the talented girls might have been tormented for their gifts as much as I was for my lack of them.

When I did start running, there was no doubt in my mind that women could run long distances—my doubts concerned my own abilities. If I wanted evidence of the strength and endurance of women, I only needed to look around me in the park or watch the faster runners shoot off at the beginning of races. In a strange way, my dismal personal log of athletic accomplishment probably helped form me as a runner. I knew I was slow from the outset and had no peak of youthful achievement to surmount. While I was wary of looking foolish, no adult embarrassment could sear my sense of self in the way being an uncoordinated teenager had. My sports ego, had it even had a moment to take shape, was nonexistent. I had nothing to lose.

I'm still a crap athlete. Whenever people ask me how fast I can run, what my best times are, it makes me laugh—I should be nobody's standard for athletic success. To find, eventually, that I could run 14 kilometers in the City2Surf spun my world around. For a woman to run for pleasure is a wildly new concept, one that isn't endorsed by any historical precedent. It was new for me too. Now, when I run it's as if I'm pushing the earth away with my feet and, with it, everything I told myself I could never do, and everything that women were told for centuries was beyond them.

5

ON THE ROAD

I ran the City2Surf in the morning, and in the afternoon I did what I now know most runners do post-race: I went to a bar and talked up my run. I pulled a wobbly chair to a sticky table and let friends who weren't runners buy me beers. In return, I put together a big story about having run 14 kilometers just after dawn.

I'd twisted my hair high into a messy knot and hooked in a pair of earrings that tinkled against my shoulders. I looked nothing like a runner; that person who'd shivered in her black shorts in the chalky morning light was just a character in a long series of anecdotes. I rolled cigarettes, and all afternoon smoke trailed around me, my bangles clattering an off-key accompaniment. For years I'd staked out these sidewalk tables at the Darlo Bar and watched runners go by in their risible shiny outfits. I'd wondered why they bothered. And here I was, an emissary returned from the realm of runners, an ethnographer set to deliver her preliminary findings.

Running yarns typically involve an elaboration of the physical and mental obstacles overcome by the runner on her way to the finish line: lessons learned, morals revealed. It had been bewildering to wait for a siren blast with tens of thousands of runners, but the run itself had lacked drama. Thanks to my overconscientious preparation, my legs were conditioned to carry me across the line—it took me a long time to grasp that usually it's possible to get away with far less training. The horror stories I'd heard about muscle seizures had made an impression too, so I had stretched for a sensible amount of time in the finish area at Bondi. I know now that a slow 14K run, even if it involves a few hills, is unlikely to provoke paralyzing muscle cramps.

Sitting on a bar chair, my legs were pleasantly sore, and though I was tired, I was hardly wiped out. All I'd had to do that morning was keep running till I passed through the inflatable tunnel that marked the finish line—and then a kid in a volunteer T-shirt gave me a medal and shrugged me in the direction of the drinks stand. I had no scars, no blisters, I wasn't even limping: so what story *did* I have to tell?

After a few beers, the bones of it fell something like this: *Ha! I'm the last person anyone ever expected to run the City2Surf and I did it. I ran all the way!* This element of surprise was what gave shape to my story, not some epic confrontation with my physical and psychological limits. I was a fish out of water, a boozy old dog learning new tricks. I'd thwarted the stereotypes about runners: it was intriguing iconoclastic me against the tens of thousands of other participants—all of whom, at least for pub purposes, behaved like the drones I needed them to be. I yammered on about the weirdos in costumes, the parents chasing their skinny-legged kids, the metal band playing on the rooftop of the Golden Sheaf, the dudes downing beers as they ran. The runner in my story was entirely subordinate to the woman at the pub; you could have been forgiven for doubting that they were the same person. The details were slipping away from me fast: I could barely remember what the cold morning air had felt like on my throat, or whether the pressure that began to sink into my hip in the last few miles retained any intensity.

I was with a forgiving circle of old friends who were point-blank impressed that I'd run 14 kilometers. They knew I wasn't an ascetic who lived and died by her gym schedule. Not one of them dampened my glee by scrutinizing my slow time. Jim, a former boxer and a unionist, asked me questions about my strength training, and the very fact that I had answers for him made me laugh. Squats and lunges, mate. I grabbed at similes: it was like being part of a moving stadium; we were lemmings, dancers, a swarm of overgrown kids chasing the Pied Piper. I knew my friends shared my skepticism about corporatized leisure, and I played to our prejudices. Was the City2Surf a dismal burlesque of contemporary life, all of us running in the same direction, obeying the rules, strapped for time—or was it a glorious celebration of the body, an electric experience of the blazing multitude? As my friend Jarrah and I waited for drinks at the bar, I reeled off yet another minor anecdote, and a guy sitting nearby chimed in. "You ran the City2Surf? Well done, love. I could never do that." I thrilled at the strangeness of being hailed as a runner in a bar, instead of just a regular

Sunday drinker. "Good to see you haven't given up on the finer things in life," he added as we picked up our beers. It got late quickly, and as I wandered home I was pleased to sense a new stiffness in my legs, a little discomfort to balance the exhilaration.

Bar talk never adds up to the whole story. I could've told a very different one that night if I'd started in India, or in Albury—or some wretched sad night, five or six or nine years earlier. Instead, I'd reveled in the endorphin-razzled flippancy of the present. The fact that I'd just had a good time with a bunch of bloody runners was something new. The maxim that we are what we repeatedly do is attributed to Aristotle. Could it be, I wondered, that the farther I ran, the merrier I'd be? What would it feel like to encounter and overcome a little more resistance? Maybe I'd simply forget the inconvenience of training and the discomfort of racing. All kinds of self-improvement fantasies made themselves available. Before I turned in for the night, I resolved to run a half marathon before the year was out.

*

This resolution proved very easy to put into practice. A week after the City2Surf, two of my cousins, Ali and Danny, suggested that we sign up to run a half marathon staged by the local triathlon club in the little town of Mudgee. This was an element in their scheme to run a marathon later that year.

People visit Mudgee for wine and food weekends, not sports. It isn't quite in the middle of nowhere, but it's a long way away from the Darlinghurst pavements where I'd held court on my training regimen. This race was selected solely for its location: the three of us lived in Newcastle, Dubbo, and Sydney, and we'd all have to travel roughly the same distance to reach Mudgee. There was just enough time for me to figure out how I was going to run even farther than I had in the City2Surf—and I agreed.

Everyone told me I needed a plan if I was going to do this: only with a plan would I make progress, and I had to make a lot of progress in under two months. I knew I couldn't train on a treadmill this time. It would take me about two hours to run a half marathon, maybe a bit longer, and I'd go mad if I stayed on a treadmill for that length of time. I had to get out of the gym. It's all about endurance, my dad's friends in Albury told me, and I said I'd take their word for it because they were triathletes, and because they'd known my father so well that their advice was stamped with his authority. If I could build my endurance, I'd be fine. *Prepare to run the distance—don't worry about your speed.* It sounded like a lesson for life. Most running tips do if you're in the market for bromides.

I started to leaf furtively through running books in sports sections and to scroll through athletics websites. It was all very well to turn up at a bar, drink four beers, and call myself a runner, but I needed practical advice. I'd taught myself how to read the Cyrillic alphabet, and I'd watched YouTube videos to figure out how to take apart an iPod or peel an artichoke. I had become proficient in living as an orphan and now I was going to teach myself how to run a half marathon. There are guides for running marathons, and there are guides to enduring grief. On the whole, the running ones are more helpful, even though I needed to duck answers to questions that I wouldn't have dreamed of asking: *Can I wear mascara when I run? What's the best footwear for running in the snow? What sort of heart monitor do I need?*

Eventually I managed to put together a perfunctory plan. Firstly, I'd undertake one long run each weekend—outdoors. This would gradually get longer week by week, and I'd hope to have run 11 or 12 miles at a stretch two weekends before starting the race. Secondly, I would aim for two or three additional, shorter runs during the week. The pundits all insisted that these involve sprints, but I had no intention of adding such indignities to my regimen. Finally, I would take my long runs and at least one weekday run outside of the gym.

I was operating on the certainty that if I stuck to my training plan, I would be able to finish this half marathon. Mostly, I did stick to it, without needing to remodel entirely the architecture of my daily life. I worked mainly as a freelancer and taught undergraduates part time so my weeks were flexible. I would make a fuss about staying home the night before a long run; the following night, I would celebrate with wine. I told my peers that I was going to run a half marathon, hoping that the prospect of failing to make good on that promise would keep me rising early.

Really, though, I didn't need a fear of public humiliation to motivate me. Running was becoming its own quiet reward, and I found the suspense it produced quite compelling. Would I be able to finish the race? Would I get there? I found myself talking a lot about running to my close friends: not just about the strange joy I'd discovered and the unexpected changes to the rhythms of my weeks, but also about the weariness and the strains, about my frequent doubt that I could make the distance.

I found myself talking more about the pain of running than I can ever remember talking about grief. Each run could have represented a stage in an allegory about recovery, endurance, or change—but it didn't have to, and as I learned to speak the language of the body, I let the metaphors sort themselves out.

Running races are linear: starting line; finish line. Fitness may be cumulative, but training isn't. The runner begins anew every time she puts on her shoes. To run at the gym had been simple: I dropped my bag beside the treadmill, draped a towel over a rail, popped a bottle of water in the designated holder, pressed a few buttons, and got going. How, then, to start running outside? I was frightened of cars, bicycles, dogs, broken sidewalks, and other people. A new set of routines emerged. Instead of running with my keys in my pocket, I'd leave them in my mailbox. I purchased a tiny MP3 player that clipped to my shorts, and I asked my friend Ben to make me a playlist. He delivered the goods: a 300-song epic that was heavy on running puns (Run DMC and Bruce Springsteen), indie '90s femme acoustic heartbreak, and dizzy early 2000s electro. I hid under a scrubby green hat, behind a pair of sunglasses, in between my headphones.

Quitting the controlled climate of the gym, I had to submit to the weather: wind, sun, clouds, and all varieties of rain between a drizzle and a downpour. Runners are supposed to train in rain, hail, or snow, but if it was bucketing down, I'd hold out for meteorological clemency. Every now and then, I'd return to the gym.

As I ran, my knowledge of the geography of Sydney was transformed. Hills are hard to avoid in the Emerald City, and their inclines are rarely regular. These undulations took on new meaning for me. Instead of tracking with my eyes the land that rises from the bays on the eastern side of the harbor up to the spine of Oxford Street, I described a lifting path with my feet. I became a moving part of the tightly controlled curves that ricochet from Woolloomooloo to the Botanical Gardens, around to the Opera House and into the lopped oblong of Circular Quay. New categories for trees presented themselves: kind trees with broad shade; trees with treacherous flowers that turn the pavement into a bright, slippery hazard; trees with bothersome hard fruits that roll underfoot like ball bearings. I kept track of the brick fences colonized by cats as snoozing spots and the gates through which friendly dogs wedged their wet noses. My own nose I stuck into other people's gardens—magnolias, waxy gardenias, all the stelliferous jasmines, lilacs, daphnes: it was winter, and I wished it were spring so that the heavy fragrant flowers might start to bloom. I stopped once to chat with a man high on a ladder, harvesting a lilli pilli to make jam; I remember him every time I run through a windfall of the pink fruit.

If I'd anticipated a dull backdrop of concrete, asphalt, and steel, this encounter with the urban biosphere, the built environment, and its human inhabitants was absorbing. I lost myself and became part of the scene. Perhaps, waiting at the traffic lights alongside a sequinned posse heading to a cocktail party—me, a study in sweat and facial flush, them, a study in fashionable zeal—I'd return to awkwardness, stare at my shoes wishing I could tap my heels together and be across the road, at the entrance to another park, and then the lights would change, and I would find myself somewhere else.

I did fret about dehydration. I ignored all the dire warnings about the effect this running might have on my knees, about overtraining, about beginner's zeal and burnout—but what if fluid shortage knocked me out? Mental images of desiccated muscles interrupted my runs; they were stripped of skin, all fluid squeezed out of them. A parched zombie runner tottered on a loop in my mind, never able to slake her thirst. This paranoia explains why my first mental running map included references to all possible drinking-water sources on my route.

To reach Rushcutters Bay Park, where I first ran, I jogged down one hill and then another to reach a narrow mossy staircase that leads into the park. Boot-camp groups use the stairs for training drills. Moss grows along the side walls here too, and it's very damp; unlike the boot-campers, I always walk down them, afraid of slipping. I knew that not far from the bottom of these stairs was a water fountain. The precious dogs of the neighborhood lapped from the dripping joint at its base. If I crossed the park, ran up a hill, turned left, and ran down a road lined with massive old fig trees and then down the other side of the hill, I'd reach another park. This one had two water fountains in the far corner. If I ran up another short, easy gradient hill and along the waterfront, I'd reach the amenities block for a tennis court and athletic fields. Inside: water.

*

Fitness enthusiasts started running to improve their health and well-being in the 1960s, but recreational running really took off around the world in the '70s. "Recreational running" is a bit of a mouthful: the correct term is definitely "jogging."

You do not stop a jogger who is jogging. Foaming at the mouth, his mind riveted on the inner countdown to the moment when he will achieve a higher plane of consciousness, he is not to be stopped. If you stopped him to ask the time, he would bite your head off.

This is how French philosopher Jean Baudrillard characterizes joggers in his book *America*. At some point, I had underlined that quote in my copy and added an exclamation mark in the margin. "Jogging" isn't a word that's so fashionable these days: it signifies a wholesomeness that lacks adventure, an earnestness without eccentricity. As I contemplated quitting the gym, I found that I too was contemptuous of jogging. I thought it spoke to a certain earnest vapidity, one that I earnestly sought to avoid—if I was going to disgrace myself by running in the park, at least I'd call myself a runner, and not a jogger.

The vocabulary of recreational running was honed and popularized in the '70s: intervals, sprints, tempo runs, fartleks, long slow-distance training, and so on. All those exasperating slogans about changing your life and feeling fabulous also have their roots in the euphoric jogging revolution. Try this: "Not long ago, Dr. Kostrubala was a fat, anxious, discontented psychiatrist. Then he discovered running. He's still a psychiatrist, but everything else in his life has been wonderfully changed." So reads the blurb to my paperback edition of the exuberant *Joy of Running*, authored by Thaddeus Kostrubala, one of the many best-selling '70s jogging guides. The cover features a smiling middle-aged couple running on grass—she's wearing a bright yellow tracksuit, he's in velvety maroon, and the zipper on his jacket is open far enough for us to see a few rogue tufts of chest hair. This couple don't look ferociously fit, they just look happy.

The Joy of Running sits on my bookshelf alongside a number of similarly buoyant volumes: *Aerobics*, by Kenneth H. Cooper ("2 million copies in print! The world's most popular physical fitness program!"); *Dr. Sheehan on Running*, by the inimitable George Sheehan ("The one book every runner must have; America's expert shows the way to total fitness and joy"); *Jogging*, by William J. Bowerman and W. E. Harris ("The simple way to physical fitness by a heart specialist and a famous track coach"); the *Van Aaken Method*, by Ernst van Aaken ("Finding the endurance to run faster and live healthier"); *Jogging with Lydiard*, by Arthur Lydiard and Garth Gilmour (the note in the flyleaf of my copy reads, "To Alison, Hope this provides the motivation—you've got the rest already there").

Most of the secondhand running manuals in my collection are low-cost paperbacks. They were written at a time when forty was well into middle age, and people worked jobs for life—or rather, male breadwinners did. They appeal to the bibliophile in me: loopy kitsch fonts, tiny text crammed to the margins of yellowing pages, awkward tables and charts, fab photos of retro running gear. Jogging became an extraordinarily popular activity extraordinarily quickly, and these books sold millions.

Whereas women were discouraged from competing in distance running events at the elite level, the jogging revolutionaries—all male, mostly doctors—made at least a little room for women. Those who competed in the women-only events organized by Avon and Bonne Bell could access a bit of training advice. It's a good example of the market rushing to meet changing social mores and the needs of a consumer group as regulations lagged.

This isn't to say that comprehensive guidance for women runners is on offer; rather, there are side observations on female physiognomy and advice about training loads. Very occasionally, a euphemistic nod to the menstrual cycle, sports bras, and pregnancy. The authors don't tend to dwell on the difficulties—child care and divorce, harassment in the workplace, everyday domestic tedium—that might have encouraged women to start running in the first place. Small concessions aside, it's assumed that the primary reader is a middle-class man with a set of manly stresses: a nagging wife at home, a bunch of kids to escape, an important job, the burden of civic responsibility. If I'd picked up one of these books when I started running, I wouldn't have recognized myself in it.

It's possible to pinpoint the year when and the city where people started jogging: Auckland, 1961. Twenty or so men gathered in a park and started running to improve their health under the supervision of a coach, Arthur Lydiard, and a cardiologist, Noel Roydhouse. For larks, they adopted the slightly archaic verb "to jog"—which was more often applied to the gait of animals—as their own, and started to run. Thus was the Auckland Jogging Club convened.

Lydiard had trained three New Zealand runners—Peter Snell, Murray Halberg, and Barry Magee—to win long- and middle-distance medals at the 1960 Rome Olympics. Now his jogging students undertook slow, steady runs and gradually increased their distances, just as I was doing. Most of them were middle-aged professional men who'd seen Lydiard speak at a local Lions Club function. They weren't interested in the peak performance ideal so prevalent in the contemporary running scene: what they wanted was to avoid a trip to the cardio ward. There's an Australian running magazine titled *Run for Your Life*. Riffs on the words "run for your life" are beloved by race organizers and the people who design T-shirts for running groups. I wrote it off as an irresistible play on words. Turns out the origins of recreational running lie with a bunch of men who were, literally, running to save their lives.

Prior to the Second World War, a heart attack was understood to be a death sentence. People who survived one were told to avoid exercise and adjust their future prospects. New knowledge about the heart changed this. Suddenly, sedentary jobs didn't represent a reprieve from manual labor: they were a dangerous lifestyle. It wasn't invisible viruses that would kill you—all those glorious bad habits would. If it's too much to claim that joggers strive for immortality, it's at least true that many of their first generation were renegotiating the boundaries of their own mortality.

Today, we take for granted that running is good for us. The language of heart health is built into the design of gyms: cardio sessions and heart-rate monitors are commonplace. When Lydiard was first putting his joggers through their paces, none of this was certain. Happily, the Auckland joggers became fitter and their hearts grew stronger. They told their friends in other cities about their successes, and jogging spread around New Zealand. On the strength of this experiment, Lydiard published his first book, *Run to the Top*, in 1962. His second book, *Run for Your Life*, published in 1965, became a global best seller.

In 1962, Lydiard was visited by Bill Bowerman, the head running coach at the University of Oregon. If at first he was interested in Lydiard's crack international athletes, he became intrigued by the Kiwi joggers and surprised to find that he couldn't keep up with them. He returned to the States and recruited a few friends to jog with him. In 1964, with his friend Phil Knight, he founded Blue Ribbon Sports, the company later renamed "Nike." There are surprisingly few steps between a bunch of unhealthy Kiwi businessmen and the establishment of what would become a global sporting-goods corporation. Bowerman's *Jogging*, another best seller, appeared in 1967 and lays out an exercise program that "will improve the level of physical fitness of nearly anyone from seven to 70."

*

The idea that running is a way of life, a mystical path to enlightenment, is frequently expressed in the books of '70s running gurus—in particular those written by George Sheehan, arguably the most famous running writer of all. If Lydiard, Cooper, and Bowerman provided the practical guidance joggers needed to get started, Sheehan gave them the wherewithal to tell a bigger story about running, one rich with allegorical resonance.

Sheehan's concept of "total fitness" encourages his readers to become that most mysterious entity, the person they want to be. He's less concerned with remodeling the physical body than with the discovery of a metaphysical self. Begin with the body, he advises, to encounter a new reality: "Become proficient at listening to your body and you will eventually hear from your essential totality—the complex, unique person you are." He was hailed by Bill Clinton as the "philosopher king of running"; Baudrillard's dig at joggers seeking higher states of consciousness is probably directed at Sheehan's acolytes. Sheehan was a strong runner, but he presents himself as a kind of everyman. He was, in fact, a New Jersey cardiologist with twelve children, a midlife convert to running—which was, he discovered, an antidote to midlife melancholy. When he started to run, he writes, "I rewrote my life story. It has become a biography of pain. I have made a career out of suffering." This kind of high-minded masochism is a constant feature of Sheehan's work, and so is the idea that running can drive a narrative of redemption.

Runner's World magazine, founded in 1966, took Sheehan on in 1970 as a columnist and medical editor, and he wrote for them about running, yearning, and suffering for twenty-five years. Books like *Dr. Sheehan on Running* (1975), *Running & Being* (1978) and *Personal Best* (1989) are peppered with training advice, but the philosophy and psychology of running are their central concerns. Sheehan's runner is an existential figure, battling bleak inner and outer worlds on the path to self-discovery. His prose is always self-deprecating, sometimes ecstatic, and occasionally bonkers. To be a successful runner, he counsels, never forget that "you are your only friend, the only protector of your body and its beauty." Although I concede that as I ran it became easier for me to think about other experiences of pain, loss, and weariness, I would have failed all the tests Sheehan set for being a committed runner. This idea of being one's only friend out there on the road speaks to a parched and lonely individualism that I find very unappealing. I enjoyed running alone, but not like this.

If Sheehan doesn't express much confidence in social bonds generally, he's also a little baffling when it comes to women runners. "When I see women running, I see a new world coming," he writes in *Running & Being*. Uh-oh. "The woman who comes to know herself to be truly a runner has discovered not only her body, but her soul as well." Sheehan is emphatically in favor of women running, not least because physical activity can dispel the "mystery" of womankind and resolve the "eternal discord between what is masculine and what is feminine." If more women ran, he concludes, the divorce rate might drop.

I imagine Sheehan's attitude to my years of delayed grief and depressed inertia would have been scathing. There are no excuses for bad living and a weak will, agree Lydiard and Bowerman: if you're fat, depressed and staring down the barrel of heart disease, you have only yourself to blame. Obviously this is out of step with contemporary thinking about the complex socioeconomic roots of what are sometimes termed "lifestyle diseases." Lydiard quotes a portrait sketched by one of his cardiologist friends: "the average middle-aged Australian is a paunchy, soft individual, probably beery, who exercises by shouting abuse on Saturday afternoons." This isn't a medical assessment, it's a moral judgment with a class slur on the side.

Runners do, I've noticed, have a tendency to take the behavioral high ground, which might be why so many people find them—or yes, us—so annoying. I've been very fit and I've been very unfit, but I'm inclined to side with the maligned sloths and loungers of the world. It may be laziness that keeps people on the couch. Then again, it may be depression, exhaustion, poverty or any one of a thousand fears and anxieties borne of complex lives. It may be that there's no one to help look after a houseful of kids.

Still, the same question lingers over all these books, one I struggle to answer: What is it that triggers the plasticity of mind required to change ingrained habits? To insist that it's just a matter of getting started is a failure of empathy that makes losers of those who can't flick a switch in their lives. For all Sheehan's interest in the total psychological experience of running, the guru who, via paperback proxies, acted as head coach to the jogging revolution isn't clear on what turns good intentions into action. Why run? Why now? A doctor's warning or an abrupt encounter with mortality might do the trick. You might suddenly find yourself running to cope with an equally sudden crisis.

The forces that nudged me into action were vague and terribly delayed, and manifested as a decision to tie some idea of myself to running a marathon. Only later did I reverse-engineer some sense into this decision; at the time, it felt random. I hopped on a treadmill and got started—but only after many, many false starts. Before that, I'd made so many other grand resolutions. Who knows why this one stuck? Perhaps Dr. Sheehan would have declared, with equanimous certainty, that I'd finally answered my calling as a runner—others had similarly cosmic explanations for what looked like a random conversion. I still haven't entirely untangled the knot of grief, rage, optimism, lassitude, and god knows what other directionless emotional energies that put me in motion.

*

These change-your-life running books promise such a simple narrative: start to run and everything will be, in Thaddeus Kostrulaba's words, "wonderfully changed." For me, it wasn't quite like that. I might have been a surprisingly easy convert to running, and I certainly enjoyed it, but I didn't suddenly unlatch myself from my bad habits. I wanted to keep doing the things runners aren't supposed to do: binge-watch TV series, drink martinis, blow afternoons in bars, smoke on balconies, lose track of time reading, and wake up in a haze. I made pledges that I'd drink no more than one glass of red the night before a long run, and then broke them. Still, I kept running, and the world began to seem kinder.

Of course, the kindness in my world wasn't solely a by-product of running. By the time I started to travel regularly and for longer stints, my sisters had grown up. Even my tiny nephew and nieces were getting bigger. By the time I started to run, the administrative catastrophe of my parents' estate had finally been put to rest.

The drab bureaucratic consequences of our parents' deaths had required me—all of us, really—to engage a numb coping mode. It had taken so long to settle the paperwork that when we sold the family home, eight years after Mum and Dad died, the window frames and architraves were clogged with cobwebs. There were jars of spices turned to dust and swollen tins of tomatoes and pears still in the cupboards; half-filled notepads, diaries and leaking pens lay scattered on the kitchen bench. None of us had stayed in the house much since the plane crash—it was just too dismal. My sisters had lived with other families, then found their own homes. There had been no question of getting tenants either: early on, the empty house took on the qualities of a mausoleum, and probate issues arose that became, let's just say, complicated.

Finally we were able to pack our childhoods into boxes and hurl the past into a huge dumpster in the driveway. Into that dumpster went the newspapers that my mother might have read one morning long ago, along with Dad's still-dusty running shoes and spare leads for the dogs. Sympathetic friends worried that detaching ourselves from the family home must be terribly traumatic—but really, by then it was a wonderful relief.

Later, as my runs out of doors became habitual, and I developed startling attachments to the streets and the parks in my Sydney neighborhood, I found a pace suited to the precarious labor of memory. I turned over images of the home that some other family now lived in, and played through tiny scenes of family life that had once left me in a raw rage. My mother standing alongside the climbing rose that grew wild over our garage and burst into thousands of tiny pink buds each spring. Were they still blooming? The roses in the front garden had been pulled out last time I drove past. My father walking toward me down the long arched corridor that split our home in two—not ours anymore, but I couldn't shake the possessive pronoun.

It was all terribly domestic: a splinter of an argument about the washing up, the view through a glass door to the back verandah, a bowl of fruit. The snail-dotted path to the washing line darkened by two majestic old camellias. The after-dinner coffee ritual that my sisters and I had been trained to administer when we were small. Why had I learned how to carry a tray full of porcelain cups and not how to grieve? I'd left home years before my parents died with the knowledge that home was intact. Why hadn't I seen its destruction coming? For the longest time, it was too dangerous to recollect my parents, let alone to miss them. Why had they let me loose on the world so young and so ill-prepared for plane crashes, catastrophes, cruelty? I ran and I wished that they were still alive and that I could go home; I told myself I couldn't and I kept running. If my skull was suddenly flooded by unmanageable emotion, I ran faster and faster until the clatter of my heart and the burn in my calves hauled me back to the present.

I needed this kind of control mechanism. *Your parents would have been so proud of you.* I heard those words so often and each time I did, I winced. It was a soppy counterfactual—the endless would-have-beens of the bereaved all are. I knew it was a grammatical black hole, but I worried awfully often about what might have been. I wasn't sure that my parents would have been thrilled that I'd ditched a law degree to study literature. I knew that the drift that had afflicted my twenties would have bothered them—even though, had they been alive to witness those years, it's unlikely I would have drifted quite so far or for so long. They would have listened patiently to my tales about catching trains across continents, but the conviction weighed heavily that they would have counseled me to follow a path closer to theirs.

I turned over the questions they would have asked me after dinner: *Why aren't you married with kids? What about knuckling down and writing this book? Shouldn't your name be on a brass plaque? How about calling it quits on this vegetarian caper? Isn't it time for your one-woman protest against the tyranny of ironing to cease?* I might have argued these points with a pair of living parents; to quarrel with ghosts requires vertiginous guesswork, and I could never be sure whether I'd finished ahead.

If, however, they'd been on the end of the phone when I was training for the City2Surf or now for a half marathon, I could be certain that my progress would have been greeted with enthusiasm. They *would* have been proud of me, delighted and probably a bit surprised. I don't recall seeing any books by George Sheehan on the shelves at home, but I know my father would have bombarded me with training tips. He loved to draw—my first driving lesson involved a three-foot-high piece of butcher's paper and an annotated diagram of the piston engine. His running advice might have started with a sketch of a skeleton festooned with arrows and calculations to show how the joints carry the body. He kept a skeleton in pieces under his desk at home, and models of hip joints and a concertina of foot bones at his office to help explain to patients what would happen to their bodies under anesthetic. Perhaps he would have used these as props: *This is where the stress will fall. This is how your weight is distributed through your foot. This bone is the one that should hit the ground first.* I would have huffed with daughterly impatience, but I wish I had been his student.

My mother would have exerted a moderating influence. *Don't exhaust yourself. Good excuse to stop drinking.* She loved to send me clippings on topics she thought would tickle my fancy, she tucked them into gossipy notes written in her neat cursive: local newspaper articles about school friends, columns from medical journals about the health of young women, recipes, photos of my sisters and our dogs, book reviews, travel stories about France. A glossy yellow box full of these letters is lodged in a cupboard, although most of the clippings have floated away. My parents both died—and this now seems incredible—without ever having had an email address, and I never once received an email from either of them. My mother, I'm sure, would have embraced the medium with enthusiasm and turned into a digital conduit for photographs, online ephemera and whatever washed up on the shores of her Internet. There would have been plenty of articles about women and running.

By the time I was ready to run the Mudgee half marathon, my grandfather, her father, did have his own email address, and he'd worked out how to open the photos I sent him. Together we looked at maps and emailed relatives on the other side of the world. Before I drove over the Blue Mountains and down to the cold plains with my aunt, he called me up to tell me not to injure myself and to be sure to get enough sleep the night before.

*

Seventy thousand people had waited with me to start the City-2Surf. In Mudgee I joined a group of under a hundred to wait for the starter's pistol beside a country sports field burnished white with overnight frost. The night before, Ali, Danny and I had crammed ourselves with pasta. To calm my nerves, I'd drunk two glasses of red, twice the dosage recommended by Tony, my father's old training partner and my number one running adviser. In the morning, we rose when it was still dark and ate more, this time bananas and honey on toast. The local triathlon club was hosting a full marathon that day too, and a small contingent of more serious-looking runners stood at the start, rubbing liniment into their calves, mostly men of the right age to be the sons of Lydiard's joggers. They reminded me of my father and his friends; I was too jumpy to pay much attention to the rest of the crowd. My cousins and I huddled together in our hoodies until the last possible moment, our bare legs pink with the cold.

When the gun was fired, there was a titter of pings as people set their watches for the race and then—silence. The course tracked dirt lanes that connected paddocks and wineries to one another, and the frost hadn't yet melted on them either. For the first few miles, I was so involved with my efforts to warm up that I forgot about the distance. I had trained in a synthetic singlet, but for the race I made a last-minute decision to wear a pink cotton T-shirt to protect my chest from the unexpected cold. (Rookie mistake: all the books are very clear that runners should never wear untested gear on race day. My shorts were new too.) Now I worried that sweat would turn my T-shirt into an icy wet blanket.

Only when I could comfortably move my fingers did I start thinking about the race. The course was mostly flat, and I ran alone and unhurried, turning over all the advice I'd been given. *You can never run too slowly. Just stick to your own pace. It doesn't matter if you have to walk for a while. It doesn't matter if you don't finish. Just keep running. Don't forget to drink water at every stop.* As the sun rose, so did a light frieze of clouds. The sky brightened and the frost melted. Warm and happy, I ran steadily. Magpies warbled, and a few sleepy cows ambled to the fence line to investigate the intruders. The distance was flagged every 5 kilometers (3.1 miles), and I ran from marker to marker with my head lifted, as if seeking a portal into that great sky, a way into the quiet landscape that sprawled around me. I raised my fingers to my neck to feel the throb of blood at my jugular, trying to connect that pulse to the sound of my feet and to the warmth in my thighs.

The moment I passed the 15-kilometer marker, everything changed. I despaired at the prospect of another 6 unvariegated kilometers. My legs lost their fluency, my muscles ached—and my new black shorts chafed against my lower back. My feet seemed to have swollen in a way they'd never swollen before, and my socks rubbed uncomfortably against the bones of my littlest toes and my ankles. I worried that my feet were bleeding, that flesh was exposed, that grit from the road was working its way into my bloodstream.

Tired and hungry, I wanted to stop running immediately. How ridiculous it was to have started at all. Was I a runner? Hardly. What was I doing stuck on a dusty road behind a vineyard in the blazing winter sun? Ali and Danny, wonderful athletes, would have finished already. Did anybody really expect me to finish? I was a joke athlete, horribly slow. I became certain that the decision to run a half marathon had been a catastrophic mistake. I started to cry. I'd wasted my time. I should have known better. I wept because I was tired and wanted some comfort. I wept big stupid sweaty sobs as I ran, and these were for my dad, and all the running tips that he couldn't give me, and for my mum, and all the loving questions that she couldn't ask. My hands felt painfully cold again, but if I stopped running, my pulse would drop and the dry air would freeze my fingertips.

My chilly hands convinced me to keep going, although I have no idea where I would have gone if I'd given up the ghost. I spluttered on, kicking stones, dripping tears and snot onto the dirt road, relieved that the field was so tiny and that this outburst hadn't been witnessed by any cheerful athletes.

Salvation appeared at the 18-kilometer drink stand, which I'd forgotten existed. The discovery that I only had 3 kilometers to go flipped my mood just as quickly as it had collapsed. Three kilometers wasn't much more than a run to the end of the park and back. As I stopped to drink a glass of sugary green soda, it became clear to me that I would make the distance, that this story wouldn't end in calamity. The man at the stand had a wiry white mustache, and I was conscious of his gaze as I gulped my soda like a little kid. "You're almost there, love," he told me. I thought I was going to burst into tears again, this time from relief. I had run much faster than I'd expected, and it struck me as hilarious, not outrageous, when an older woman with water bottles strapped to her hips sprinted past me in the last straight before the finish and, effectively, beat me. Incredulous, delighted, I let my legs take me all the way across the line and hugged my aunt when I got there.

That afternoon we drove back to Sydney, and when we arrived I was too tired to work out a pub spiel. My legs had cramped up in the car, and I held a banister for support as I hobbled up the stairs to my front door. I called my sisters and grandfather, and told them that I'd finished. I had no rococo details to add: it was me and a finish line. Cold baths are supposed to be good for muscle strain, but I ran a hot bubble bath and twisted myself into it with no confidence that I'd be able to haul myself out when it cooled.

6

TELLING TALES

Turn on the TV. A woman is jogging alone in a forested park. It's early morning, and we know that there, in the forbidding darkness on the other side of the trees, is danger. We've all seen this clip before, or something like it. It never glows with a buttery morning light. No, the sky is cold and clinical. The camera follows the runner—maybe we hear the accelerated rhythm of her breath and the regular *thump-thump* of her feet. We can't see ourselves from this angle when we run, but it's hard not to contemplate how we might look to a predator, or to a camera. Is this runner safe? If she turns her head and we glimpse her face, we can see that she's lost in her run.

And then, something catches her eye. She spots it before we do. She stops, and there in the bushes lies the body of another woman. She's dead. She's dying. She's been brutalized. This is what happens to women who go jogging alone. The runner pulls out her phone and calls for help.

The website TV Tropes has a stand-alone category named "Joggers Find Death." It's a staple opening scene for hourlong episodes of crime dramas, and a quick way both to present a corpse and to seed general paranoia about the safety of public places. If we're trained in narrative conventions—that is, if we've watched a lot of TV—we know the scene can go another way: the runner gets clobbered and is dragged into the bushes by an unseen assailant. It's an effective device because the discourse that running alone can be dangerous for women is so well established. Nina Kuscsik—one of those who, in the early '70s, campaigned vigorously for women to be recognized as U.S. marathon entrants—often recalls in interviews being hailed by police patrols when she was training. Why? The cops assumed someone was chasing her. Breaking with convention put her body on display. The tense female jogger who finds a corpse (or becomes one) is one of the latest additions to a long, complex visual history insisting that if a woman is running, trouble is brewing. She should watch out, we're taught: someone might be watching, and that someone might be dangerous.

I've never been attacked while running, thank god, and if someone's trailed me, I haven't noticed. This isn't to say that I've been anything but highly conscious of the spaces in which I've run. I've been catcalled running past pubs and let smart-ass comments about my body crumble behind me. I've stone-walled sleazy conversational overtures at traffic lights, and I've pretended not to hear what men in cars have shouted at me. Without my running shoes on, I've been followed home from bars and experienced terrible jitters on empty streets late at night. I've jolted at shadows and made loud, imaginary cell phone calls to ward off vicious imaginary attackers. Don't rush, that's the folk wisdom. Don't let anyone know you're scared. If the tapping heels of your shoes echo on the asphalt, don't make it worse by speeding up.

It's hard to separate the rational fears from the confected ones, but they all turn on a sense that a woman looks vulnerable when she runs, whether in a marathon or back home at night. In many parts of the globe today, women's disadvantage can still be measured by restrictions on their movement and visibility. In Pakistan in 2005, fifty women were arrested for trying to run a marathon—to run, to appear as a body in public, can be dangerous. Although She Runs the Night skirted political matters, in some women-only running events, the link between bodily freedom and running is clearly marked, from the Thelma & Louise Women's Half Marathon that's held in Utah each year, to the Casablanca Women's Run and the Beirut Marathon Women's Race.

The most notorious case of violence against a woman runner is that of Trisha Meili, better known as the Central Park Jogger, who was gang-raped in Manhattan's Central Park in 1989. That case generated tremendous media attention; five men were quickly and wrongfully convicted of the crime, and didn't have their convictions overturned for many years. In her 1991 essay on the attack and its aftermath, Joan Didion asks why this particular story was reported with such enthusiasm when thousands of other violent crimes against women pass without media comment. The Jogger, Didion argues, was idealized in terms of her gender, race, and class: the white, middle-class victim of a crime committed, or so it was thought, by poor men of color. This tale was so easy to tell that most commentators, afflicted by a bout of chivalric blindness, failed to scrutinize the credibility of the case against the men. As Didion writes, "stories in which terrible crimes are inflicted on innocent victims . . . have long performed as the city's endorphins, a built-in source of natural morphine working to blur the edges of real and to a great extent insoluble problems."

That's not only true in New York City. In the case of the Jogger, a miscarriage of justice was overshadowed by the confirmation in public opinion that running involves an element of risk for women. This isn't to argue that violence against women runners never happens. In 2015, an eighteen-year-old woman from the Australian town of Bendigo went missing while jogging and was found, distressed, twenty-four hours later. Too often, though, a woman running alone is taken to signify both risk and irresponsibility—as if to strike out on your own is to ask for trouble or, at least, to invite objectification. *Is it safe?* we ask ourselves, and we can never be certain of the answer.

When a young woman named Masa Vukotic was found stabbed to death in a Melbourne park in 2015, a senior policeman was widely quoted in the media as warning women to avoid being in these kinds of public spaces on their own. He later revised his comments, advising women merely to "be aware of their circumstances" but the core message remained: women must be vigilant; women must take responsibility. When, six weeks later, a young woman was gang-raped at knifepoint in Albury, my hometown, the mayor claimed that women walking the streets by themselves at night were issuing an "invitation" to attackers. These comments rightly sparked outrage. To me, it sounded as if these powerful men were saying that a woman alone in a public space is asking for trouble. I often walked the streets of Albury on my own at night after Mum and Dad died; I didn't learn to drive until I was thirty-three. Did the mayor and the policeman wish for a return to the days of chaperones, curfews, and dress codes? Like many others, I wondered why they didn't speak directly to the men who attack women in parks, and tell them to stop.

*

Going for a run shouldn't feel like a performance. Often, it does. Women get looked at—ogled, appraised, admired, gazed upon with adoration, spied on—all day and all night. Women runners aren't all the same, of course. We're not united by some essential experience of womanhood, but we do have to endure this visibility. As trans activist Julia Serano writes, "the one thing that women share is that we are all perceived as women and treated accordingly." Cue some bonehead in the park yelling a comment about boobs.

Decades have passed since it's been established that women can run marathons without damage to themselves (or to the patriarchy), yet everyone has a view on what women runners should look like. Depending on whom you listen to, women runners are either too thin, too fat, too masculine, or too muscled. Runners' faces are too gaunt, their bodies are too sunburned; they've lost their gorgeous curves, or they're carrying too much weight. With their hair scraped back and their sweaty faces, women who run are insufficiently feminine. It's as if they're not making an effort. Their breasts look weird, their calves are thick, they should have been able to run off their post-baby stomachs. Women runners are too sexy, in their skimpy little outfits (*Why doesn't she cover up?*) and not sexy enough, too strong to simper (*Doesn't she know men are threatened by strong women?*). Even if you're not running for male attention—and my guess is that most women runners aren't—it's hard to evade these norms. *Why is she out there on her own? Doesn't she know it's dangerous?* ask the moralists. *What is she doing to herself? Doesn't she want to have kids?* worry the catastrophists. *Why shouldn't I stare at her? She's out in public. She loves it,* insist the dickheads.

What I wanted to look like when I ran was invisible. I didn't want to be available for casting in any of these narratives. That's why a shadowy gym was initially such a refuge. Some people enjoy being on display, but not me. I really did want to blend into my surroundings, to throw off the awareness that I was being looked at. This wasn't just my own neurosis, but one that many women around me carry. "I could never run like you do," a friend told me. "I'd look like a complete idiot." I hear women worrying about looking fat, awkward, sweaty, and ugly. The desire to run unnoticed is a common note in memoirs by women runners, whether they're champions or casual athletes.

It's too easy to write off concerns like these as a matter of silly female vanity or overconscientiousness about personal safety. It's exhausting to have absorbed such demands about how we appear to the world. They can slow a woman down; they can stop you altogether. To run in public, I had to convince myself that no one was paying any attention to my gait, that no one was whispering about my heavy thighs, that my sweaty face was uninteresting to strangers, that anyone who bothered to scoff was a fool, that nobody was following me. I wanted to run for long enough to leave all these worries behind, to find a path out of narratives about vulnerability and danger. I wanted to forget what I looked like and to feel nothing more than my limbs moving against the air and the weight shifting from the ball to the heel of my foot as I moved forward.

Fun runs, half marathons, and get-fit-quick runs aren't the only reasons women run. If that woman running alone in the early morning were wearing heels and a dress, even more narrative possibilities would open up: Is she scared, drunk, running out on a lover? We'd be worried about her. If it were at sunset, she might be late for a show, possessed by inexplicable glee, trying to hail a cab. We'd wonder whether someone was chasing her, or whether she was in a pushy rush. A mother might run after a two-year-old in a park; a lover might run home late at night, humiliated and disappointed; someone else might run along the sidewalk without an umbrella on a rainy afternoon. Women figure disproportionately among the refugees of the world; to leave an abusive relationship, you need somewhere to run. We may choose to run marathons but we do not choose to run like this.

Is there a danger in conflating recreational running with more urgent acts of flight? They're not the same—obviously—but the way we look at women runners is primed by how other women on the run are presented more broadly: vulnerable, powerless. Running for pleasure can be a safe simulation of these desperate flights, one that conditions the physical and mental strength that may be required in a time of danger. *Run like someone's chasing you*, advise the motivational guides. But what if someone really *is* chasing you? The language of running twists and warps so that it can be hard to tell.

*

I still find it hard to call myself a runner without quickly adding a few qualifications: I'm very slow, not at all athletic, nothing like those *other* runners, you wouldn't have picked it if I hadn't told you, right? I might add, What I really am is a reader.

"Television rots your brain," my father always insisted. He hated the cheap tropes of serial TV; like some latter-day Adorno, he thought they deadened the spirit, although his concern was less with the revolutionary spirit of his daughters than their work ethic. My mother worried about what the violence on TV might do to us. The parental will held and, as a result, I spent very little time in front of a small screen when I was a kid. Those crime shows with the creepy stalker camera intros? I wouldn't have seen a single episode until I was halfway through my teens. Books shaped my ideas about the world; books shaped my ideas about myself. ("You live in books and you don't know anything about the real world," complained a boyfriend whom I failed to recognize as a textbook dud.) I read walking to school, I read after class, I read under the covers with a broken light from a dollar store clipped to my paperback.

"You always did have your nose in a book," my grandfather said when I enrolled in graduate school, as if he'd known all along where I was heading. I kept reading, and it turned into something like my job. For the best part of a decade, I stood in front of undergraduates and tried to convince them that no scrim separates literature from the world, that language and life are intermediaries, that the stories we tell about the world bring new worlds into being. Even though our discussions often wandered, I never spoke with my students about running; I could well have asked them to examine how crime shows and newspaper reports about attacks on women runners frame public spaces and female bodies, and so define them.

I was still teaching when I started to run and, of course, just as I noticed women running on TV, I also began to pay attention to the women runners who crossed the pages I was reading: nymphs tearing away in fright in Ovid's *Metamorphoses*; Daphne on the run from Apollo. Aemylia in *The Faerie Queen* is captured by a savage man after running away with her lowly born lover; she tells her story to another captive, Amoret, and warns her that the man will rape her. Amoret flees, "her fear a spur to haste her flight."

Hot messes run because they're out of control, terrified floozies run because they've done something silly. Scenes from favorite novels returned to me: F. Scott Fitzgerald's lovelies hurtle around, crazed and drunk; Robin Vote in *Nightwood* is restless, won't stay still: these women are trouble, especially to their lovers, and they're also clearly marked as troubled. Runaway girls may have adventures in fiction, but they tend to wind up back home, redomesticated. (Turn on the radio and tune into all those pop laments about run-run-runaway babes and girls: *Why-why-why did she leave? Who took her home? Was it her father or another man?*)

There are exceptions—Athena and the warrior goddesses of the ancient world; Atalanta, outrunning her suitors—but, in a disheartening premonition of the newspaper reports and TV shows about the danger that women runners put themselves in, most of the literary women I encountered were trying to escape belligerent, abusive, and threatening men. Literary-minded sports officials could point to the canon and say, look, it's always been like this.

As I reread canonical works of fiction that popped up on the syllabus, especially those authored by women, I looked for the runners. Sturdy characters, such as Elizabeth Bennet, go walking—but can we picture her upping and running around Pemberley? The unhappy and adulterous Emma Bovary runs away from Charles's house in Tostes; Tess of the d'Urbervilles runs on the moors. Running determines the fate of unruly Judy in *Seven Little Australians*: running away from home prefigures her death; she later runs to save her little brother and is crushed by a falling tree.

Sometimes running away is a metaphor, but still it's synonymous with hardship: Elizabeth Bennet's little sister suffers the consequences of her elopement, and Fanny's mother in *Love in a Cold Climate* is branded "the Bolter" because of her flightiness. The escape of Sethe from slavery in Toni Morrison's *Beloved* is traumatic. Tragic bodies, bodies of confined women, the defiled bodies of women who didn't run fast enough, repressed bodies that never knew pleasure, fearful bodies, bodies that were property and so had to be controlled. Maybe it's familiarity with this grim parade of bodies that prompts spectators to see something wrong with women who run.

I borrowed anthologies of running literature from the library, hoping there were some obvious examples I'd missed. The anthologies confirmed that there are surprisingly few depictions of women running in literary history, and certainly none that treat running as an easy declaration of physical vitality. The editors of running anthologies don't comment on the fact that distress and disgrace are the common themes that bring women runners in literature together. Instead, they devote their analyses to the many breeds of male runners we encounter in epic poetry, ballads, novels, and films.

For men, running can serve many narrative purposes. Men run to hunt, for sport, to chase women, to escape the humdrum, to seek fame and fortune, even for the pleasure of movement. The sun falls on their bodies, the wind speeds their heels. Where was the glory of the female body in motion? Where were the women running because it feels good, or to get somewhere they want to go, or to express a desire for even greater freedom? For every warrior queen (there aren't a hell of a lot of them *and* most meet a gory end), there are many more terrified damsels being hunted.

Screens big and small offer us a few alternatives—but they too require quick qualification. For every *Run Lola Run* showing a feisty babe running through the city, there are a hundred screaming cheerleaders being chased through a forest by a cartoon predator, and usually because they've fucked or flirted with the wrong guy. Even when tough, uncompromising female characters, such as Clarice Starling and Claire Underwood, go running in *Silence of the Lambs* and *House of Cards*, the very fact that they run alone confirms their outsider status; their tense features show us that they are alert to danger. These are roads to nowhere.

In the literary traditions in which I was schooled, as in history, women are rarely free to roam. I should not have been as surprised as I was to discover that women in literature didn't enjoy the freedom of movement that I did. The key trope of the madwoman in the attic, as elaborated by feminist literary historians Sandra Gilbert and Susan Gubar, figures the patriarchal confinement of the woman artist; confinement and restriction is also the fate of women who seek mobility. And that's not all.

In a cruel twist of patriarchal logic, if running is represented as bad news for women, many literary women suffer because they are unable to run, no matter how dire their marriages or cruel their families. The social situation of women—particularly middle-class women—keeps them in place. We would cheer if Dorothea Brooke left the drippy curate Casaubon, but George Eliot makes it painfully clear in *Middlemarch* that she cannot. The same goes for the orphaned sisters Laura and Clare, stuck in a prison of dependence controlled by Laura's husband in Elizabeth Harrower's *The Watchtower*. Trapped by circumstance, the girls simply cannot leave. Disobedient women run and suffer the consequences; good women stay home and they suffer too.

I didn't want to get mired in marriage dramas and morality tales about women knowing their place. I wanted bodies that told stories that weren't about fear and escape. I wanted acknowledgment of sensations that lie outside of these plots: sunshine, unloosened hair, a quickened pulse, flushed cheeks. If these pleasures sound decidedly post-coital, that's because women's mobility and sexuality have been closely linked—and controlled—in literature as in the world. There's no etymological basis for the sonority between "chased" and "chaste," yet there's a snarl of unmissable, often contradictory connections in literature between running and women's sexuality. Women run when they are chased; women must run from predators to stay chaste. It is not natural for women to run unless they're chased; chaste women have no need to run.

For me, running was nothing like this. When I began to run, my understanding of the significance of my body in the world shifted. I grasped the link between despair and immobility at both an intellectual and embodied level: for years I'd been stuck in grief, convinced that my body lacked the eloquence for anything but sadness. My imagination blunted by escapist fantasies, I'd wallowed and boozed and cried to sound that long, droning song. But when I started running, was I writing a new narrative of despair with my feet? Was anybody chasing me then? Hardly. I'd endured the consequences of some poor romantic decisions, but I'd managed to walk out of those situations. In putting my sneakers on, I wasn't fleeing those ex-lovers, I was running into an entirely different storyline, one that had nothing to do with bad romance. I discovered how transformative it could be to run for hours with no consequences but sore legs, a lighter mood, and an appetite. My sense of where I could go and how I could move was reconfigured; the alarmism about women runners struck me as ludicrous. Sure, there was plenty I wanted to leave behind, but running wasn't a sign of crisis—it was part of the movement, sometimes vigorous, sometimes cautious, toward recovery.

*

As I bandied around my thesis that women in literature don't run unless they're in strife, I was frequently reminded of the mythological figure of Atalanta, the hunter who swore an oath of virginity to Artemis. "What about Atalanta?" a Shakespeare scholar rebuked me. "What do you mean powerful, happy women don't run? Now there's a runner for you. *She* should lead your discussion."

And so: Atalanta. She appears many times in Greek mythology as a hunter, an athlete, and even as a crew member on the *Argo*. In one version of her story, she was abandoned at birth and suckled by a bear. In Robert Graves's telling of the Caledonian boar hunt, Atalanta, "the swiftest mortal alive," draws first blood with a "timely arrow." She was as celebrated for her beauty as for her speed. Through the ages, the combination of her bravery and her resistance to marriage have fascinated artists—with the bizarre culmination of this being her incarnation as the hood ornament on Studebaker cars. I won't go into the contested versions of the stories that led Atalanta to be reunited with her father, or his decree—against the advice of no lesser an authority than the Delphic Oracle—that she must marry. Her athletic prowess couldn't free her from this patriarchal expectation. Atalanta was able to impose one condition: she would only marry the man who could best her in a footrace. In the story of the golden apples, many suitors perish in the effort to outrun Atalanta. One young man, Hippomenes, is scornful of their efforts—until he sees her move. He appeals to Aphrodite for help, and the goddess of love intercedes, giving him three enchanted golden apples. Hippomenes rolls these onto the course, distracting Atalanta. As the virgin gathers love's apples—of course she can't resist them, what woman could fight her desire for such rare fruits?—she is passed by Hippomenes. He crosses the line first, wins the race, and, in spite of her protestations, wins the maiden. It's as if every woman, no matter how withholding, no matter how defiantly fast, is waiting to be seduced.

If Atalanta was defined first by her virginity and her extraordinary hunting skills, her story culminates in this marriage, the key narrative device for representing women's experiences. Spinster, old maid, widow, bride, wife: how difficult it is to relinquish these categories. Atalanta may have been a wonderful runner—but she is also the trophy bride offered to the winner of a race. Her wishes about marriage count for little. Ultimately, Atalanta takes her place in a story about the restoration of a gendered order. As mesmerizing a runner as she is, I'm not convinced her story inaugurates a narrative tradition of the liberated female body.

I did once see a marriage proposal delivered from the sidelines of a running race. A man stood waiting patiently for his beloved to run past. He brandished a six-foot-high sign bearing an enormous image of the woman's face and the question, "Will you marry me?" A bit like an advertisement for a photocopy service. This poor woman must have been puffing her guts out somewhere behind me on the course; the runners around me cheered in encouragement to the guy as they ran by. I kept running and mused on her likely reaction. She was probably thrilled when she reached him—I hope so—but I would have been mortified to see myself reflected like this as I ran. She must have trained to complete the event, as I had, and looked forward to the run as a major occasion in her year.

I remember that the sun was gleaming like a beacon, that it was surprisingly hot and the crowd in good humor. Instead of drinking it all in, instead of celebrating the ground moving beneath her feet, one woman had to contemplate a marriage proposal, as if one of Aphrodite's apples had been rolled onto the course. Couldn't she have been allowed to finish her race, celebrate her run, and then consider the future? What if she didn't want to marry him? I wondered the same thing about Atalanta, even though her story was told long before the tropes of romantic love were set in place.

I've no idea whether the proposal I saw was accepted, although maybe I could dig into an online forum and find out. Maybe the woman took Atalanta as her role model and said, "Yes ... but only if you can beat my time in this race." Or maybe she accepted—and then had to squeeze an engagement ring onto her swollen finger before she kept running. I've no reason to doubt that this placard proposal was sincere and loving. If the marriage came off, may they still be a happy couple. Still, I can't help but think that it was all terribly ill-timed. Matrimony!—and just as a girl is caught up in a vivid and intense display of independence and physical activity.

Is marriage the only happy ending for a woman runner? Cautionary tales about the sorry lot of women who run still linger in our shared cultural spaces. What an astonishing breach there is between their agonized depictions and the lived experience of women running in the contemporary Western world. Transformation, escape, recovery—these are all destinations we can reach by running. Most women runners aren't in danger. Maybe some started out angry, hurt, despairing—I did—but running can be a repudiation of that pain, rather than its prolongation.

Novelist and marathon runner Joyce Carol Oates writes, "If there's any activity happier, more exhilarating, more

nourishing to the imagination, I can't think what it might be."
Expressions by women of the sheer delight that is being in motion are a notably recent phenomenon—and I wish I'd heard
more of them when I was forming my ideas about my body
and its limits. Enough stressed and vulnerable women in parks,
I say. Enough with fleeing maidens and distressed damsels.
What my journals and notebooks record is the movement from
anxiety to invigorated glee, the discovery that my body can
tell stories that haven't been written. Running hasn't taken me
into or out of matrimony. No, for me, running became a narrative end in itself—and I suppose if you find yourself confronted
by a set of stories that don't fit, you have to tell your own.

7

LOOK AT HER GO

There is glamour running gear, high-performance running gear, comfort running gear, sexy running gear, yoga goddess running gear. There is running gear that says, *I am trouble*, shirts that tease, *Catch me if you can*, ensembles that warn, *Don't even bother*, shoes that insist, *This woman is fast*. I don't think there's any running outfit that I could imagine for myself, at least not one that I'd want to run in, that I wouldn't be able to buy somehow.

Not so long ago, however, women runners needed to improvise to dress themselves. Women's running shoes weren't in production when Kathrine Switzer and Bobbi Gibb tackled the Boston Marathon; then, as I've said, runners made do with crepe-soled shoes designed for other purposes. If they could find a good fit, they ran in men's or boys' shoes. The photographs in those 1970s running guides show women in moccasins, tennis shoes, and espadrilles.

Male runners didn't have a whole lot of footwear choices either—but at least they didn't have to work out what to do with their breasts. When jogging was on the rise in the 1960s, there was no such thing as a sports bra. Women who wanted to avoid the uncomfortable sensation of bouncing bosoms and the leering they attracted were out of luck. A "free swing" tennis bra was on the market in the United States in 1975, and a sports bra was patented in 1979. Women were already competing in tennis, sprinting, horseback riding, and most other sports at the highest of levels. How did busty women make do? Why do more women run now than in the '70s, and why does the ratio of female to male marathoners and half marathoners continue to rise? A few decades of innovation in corsetry shouldn't be discounted as a contributing factor.

If we dart back a few centuries, we find the beginning of a vivid argument in favor of movement-arresting sports bras. Smock races were a common feature of village sports carnivals in the British Isles from the seventeenth to the nineteenth century. In these events, women sprinted short distances for the prize of a piece of clothing, usually a smock. It was not frowned upon for runners to compete lightly clad and with their breasts unbound. There's a dash of ye olde wet T-shirt contest here. Crowds would travel from nearby villages to watch the action— and they weren't there for displays of female athleticism.

In England, smock races spawned a subgenre of pervy pastoral poetry, the smock poem, in which B-grade poets praised the delights of watching women's breasts jiggle as they ran.

When I wrote that I struggled to find women runners in literature, I neglected to mention this marginal genre, which illumi-
nates another way audiences watch women run. Where crime
TV says that a woman running alone is in danger, the smock
poem and its descendants insist that women's bodies are made
for entertainment.

The best-known smock poem is probably "The Smock-
Race, at Finglas," which appeared without attribution in a
1714 volume of *Poetical Miscellanies*. The "panting Rivals,"
three village girls named Oonah, Nora, and Shevan, compete
for a "smock enrich'd with Lace" before an audience of rogues,
young squires and Dubliners. You can practically hear the poet
panting along with the runners. He attributes to the goddess
Venus an intervention that unties the strings of Nora's petti-
coat: she loses the race when she stops to knot them. Oonah
makes no such concession to modesty: "Stript for the Race how
bright did she appear!/ No Cov'ring hid her Feet, her Bosom
bare, /And to the Wind she gave her flowing Hair." Behold the
topless runner! And thus Oonah wins the race, the smock, and
the hand in marriage of a handsome swain named Felim. The
poem closes, "The Smock she won a Virgin, wore a Bride."
As with the story of Atalanta and the three golden apples, the
happy ending is a marriage.

British comedians have done their best to keep the cultural
legacy of the smock races alive. In a skit in Monty Python's
1983 film *The Meaning of Life*, for example, a man sentenced to
death for the crime of telling gratuitous sexist jokes is allowed
to choose the manner of his execution. He elects to be chased
off a cliff by a group of half-naked women. A crowd of topless runners, whose helmets and wristbands match their bikini

bottoms, administer the sentence. No sports bras here. It's filmed in slow motion, and close-up shots of bouncing knockers are cut between footage of the condemned man running for his life. *Boobs! Boobs! Boobs!* It's incredibly silly—but also a vexing reminder that even though the rules on women's participation in sports had been loosened by the 1970s, other social deterrents existed. If you can't ban women from running, then you can always just laugh at them. Benny Hill's stable of topless women are there to be snickered at, especially when they chase him around the park. *Bounce! Bounce! Bounce!* I don't think I'm the only runner to dread being the object of this kind of schoolboy eroticization. It may be that women wear sports bras as much to avoid being mistaken for lost competitors in smock races or extras in a Benny Hill skit as for comfort.

*

The nonexistence of the sports bra has not been a problem for male artists who, on the whole, have preferred to paint women naked and sedentary. To speak in the broadest of terms, in the history of Western painting, as in the history of literature, women rarely run—and when they do, they are in trouble. What this means is that women who run for pleasure are defying a long visual history that equates female flight with disobedience, distress, and trouble. It goes at least some way to explain why shock was the response to images of Switzer and Gibb.

There is a painting by Sandro Botticelli hanging in the Prado in Madrid, the first of the Nastagio degli Onesti series, that shows how tightly knotted ideas about gender and running can be. In this painting, a woman is running for her life.

She doesn't have a half marathon in her sights; she's clearly not running to keep fit. It's too late for her to turn and look to see whether she's got a chance to get away, because a hunting dog has leaped up and taken her thigh between his jaws. Streaming behind her naked body, first a blaze of golden curls, and then a knight on a rearing horse, his grand scarlet cape billowing like a bloodied sail. Unlike Botticelli's more famous *Venus*, the serene face of a thousand fridge magnets and wedding invitations, this beauty has taken flight—and the knight's sword is raised high to strike her down. In a cross-genre mash-up with a crime show, this scene would precede the discovery of her body in the woods.

There's an onlooker: a young man in red hose. His name is Nastagio degli Onesti, and his broken heart is the trigger for a frightening cautionary tale to runaway ladies. I was terribly startled by this painting when I first saw it while loafing around Madrid. All I'd wanted to do on that trip was to meander through galleries during the day, and through streets and plazas at night, caught in that pleasant zone between being lost and purposefully adrift. I walked around the stately Retiro gardens each morning before sitting down to coffee and trying to persuade myself that the next day, I would run a few laps. It was an off period in my running, and the drive to get moving had disappeared. Daily I was defeated by the conviction that I would stick out, that I would look strange if I ran. No one else was running and, not being made of the same stuff as those running pioneers, I didn't have it in me to be the first.

As I traipsed again through the Prado, I had running on my mind, which might be why this painting of a woman runner in distress stayed with me. Why was she running? Why wasn't

I? It wasn't until I returned to Sydney that I started to make sense of it. I took a magnifying glass to the library and peered at a plate of the scene in a heavy book on Renaissance painting. Small details: bleeding scratches on the woman's ankle and arms; the curve of her belly; a white goat grazing placidly in the middle ground; the golden studs on the trappings of the elegantly poised horse. The woman is arranged in the classic pose of the runner, with one foot ground into the earth as if to draw from it energy to propel herself away from the sword.

Nastagio appears three times on the canvas, each a step forward in time. First, he's a tiny figure in the background, almost imperceptible. Next, a slightly larger Nastagio decamps to the corner of the frame, where he's utterly absorbed in contemplation. But the Nastagio who demands our attention is in the clearing, watching the knight and the woman. His expression is that of a startled man who doesn't quite know what to do. He makes a perfunctory shoo-shoo movement with a stick to fend off the hunting dog.

It's not unusual to hear the pursuit of love phrased as a man hunting a woman; here, that metaphor is displayed in graphic terms, the woman unambiguously prey to the knight. And for many authors of running guides, the primal running scene is, in fact, the hunt. Recreational running is repurposed as a kind of practical activity, at least for men: chasing food, feeding the kids meat, and kicking along the evolutionary can. An origins-of-running scene is a set-piece in most of the 1960s and '70s running manuals that I've read. These tableaux depict imaginary Paleolithic nuclear families—the father goes off to chase antelopes, and the mother stays in the cave to look after the kids and gather some grains. Best-selling contemporary writers, such as Bernd Heinrich and Christopher McDougall, are still preoccupied with the hunters of early human cultures and their capacity to chase down ruminants. The argument goes that it's natural for humans to run, we were born to do it, and so we should just get out there and run. Not all Paleolithic anthropologists agree with this analysis, nor with its framing of the family lives of early humans. For women runners, the immediate problem with this man-as-hunter line is that it provides no satisfactory evolutionary fairy tale to fall back on. If men run because they have ancient hunting blood in their veins, why do women run? Must we return *again* to the answer: because someone is chasing them, because they're breaking some biologically determined code of gender conduct? Soon, we find ourselves stuck in a briar patch of acculturated ideas about men chasing women in the heat of passion, men chasing women for their own good, men chasing women to restore the natural order. And so it's hard work to push back against a tradition of representation that insists if a woman is running, she's fair game.

*

Why is the woman in Botticelli's painting being chased? It's because she refused a man. If there's any kind of running that's worrisome to the patriarchal status quo, it's skipping out on a fiancé, husband, or father. Botticelli borrowed the story from Boccaccio's *Decameron*, a fourteenth-century set of bawdy morality tales told by travelers holed up in a castle. This one deals with renegade virtue and romantic opportunism. (It didn't make the cut for inclusion in Pasolini's 1971 film version of the *Decameron,* a romp heavy on the screams, gasps and moans.) Unhappy Nastagio leaves his home in Ravenna for a bit of soul-searching after his advances were spurned by a capricious woman. Walking in the forest, he comes upon the gruesome scene painted by Botticelli: "a young Damosell come running toward him, naked from the middle upward, and her faire skinne rent and torne with the briars and brambles . . ."

Botticelli tells the tale over four panels. In the second, we see the knight kneeling over the fallen woman, tearing her body open. Renaissance audiences familiar with the *Decameron* would know that the knight and his prey are both phantoms. The knight, Guido degli Anastagi, bids Nastagio stay and listen to his story. The fallen woman is bound to him by a curse, says Anastagi. In life, she rejected him. Crushed, he committed suicide, and the wicked woman set to "rejoycing immeasurably in mine unhappy death." He was condemned to eternal punishment for his suicide, and she was condemned to join him in the afterlife to suffer the consequences of her flightiness. We never learn her name or why she denied the knight. The curse: every Friday, degli Anastagi must chase the woman through the forest, slash her back open with the dagger he'd used to end his life, then rip out her heart and feed it to his dogs. It's a hideous, histrionic revenge fantasy; today, a jilted lover might run a marathon instead to get over it.

Nastagio is shocked—until he realizes that he can turn the spectacle to his own ends. He invites the woman who walked out on him, Bianca Traversari, to dine in the forest the following Friday so that they can watch the phantom knight strike down the cruel strumpet. Bianca gets the message: stick with your man. The final panel is a wedding scene. The bride, Bianca the white, her perfect Renaissance features a blank, stays seated. Is she dreaming of running off to another lover, of a life without the feckless Nastagio and his gaudy red hose? The paintings were commissioned in 1483—as a wedding present.

Taken together, Boccaccio's story and Botticelli's painting demonstrate the powerful link that we've already encountered between the image of a woman running and cultural sanction. If running off is the action of a woman who seeks sexual autonomy, it is also her punishment. The ghost woman didn't start off by running; she just said, "No, thanks." Her impropriety was to imagine that she could love whom she pleased—which made the knight start chasing her. The painter has captured her running, an eternal signal of her impropriety. She *must* have broken the rules. Run, ladies, and you will be run to ground.

Is it too much to claim that paintings over five hundred years old have any bearing on runners today? I don't think so. What Botticelli's runner shows us is that the uneasiness about the idea of women running experienced by sports officials in the early twentieth century had very deep roots, that the worried depiction of women runners across literary history is consistent with patterns in other art forms. It tells us about the everyday history of women running and how that's tied to autonomy. Umpteen variants of this story operate around the core of a woman being punished—through violence, mockery, exile—for running in the wrong place, alone and without protection. It's never neutral for women to run.

As the story of the nameless female runner and her fierce, angry antagonist unfolded before me, I mused on whether images like this lay at the foundation of my grandmothers' worries about unladylike behavior. Could it be that the warnings

of the *Decameron* about the impropriety of running had fueled
my sense that running wasn't for me?

*

Botticelli's runner is naked, and that makes the Nastagio
paintings all the more shocking. There's no costume to protect
her. She's condemned to being chased by the knight as Nastagio and everyone who visits the Prado stares at her.

We don't know what Melpomene wore when she tried
to run the Olympic marathon in 1896, but the conventions
around what women runners look like have changed pro-
foundly. Throughout the twentieth century, women have been
required to cover less and less of their bodies, especially when
playing sports. Running gear makes it easier to interpret why
a woman is running. There's now a truly astonishing array of
items to help us declare what kind of runners we are. Consumption offers a quick and shallow means of reinventing the
self. Shorts and sneakers say, calm down, I'm just out for a run.
An uber-femme running outfit might baffle the spectator as to
whether a runner is embracing conventional ideas about femininity or subverting them. There are running outfits for women
who want to look high-tech and in charge; there are frilly pink
skirts and leopard-print shorts for those who want to look
foxy; presumably there's a way to combine both modes. Stella
McCartney has designed a range of pricey running gear for
Adidas. Retro runners can model their wardrobe on the cute
shorts that Grete Waitz and Josephine Hanson wore when they
were breaking records in the '70s. To cover up from the sun
and prying eyes, athletes can wear head-to-toe compression

gear; alternatively, plenty of women commune with the sun by running in tiny bra-and-shorts combos. A runner can literally buy into the peak performance narrative through the acquisition of costly "technical" garments that promise to boost her endurance. How could anyone think that women runners were vulnerable when there's all this choice available? Consumer goods aren't a pathway to self-actualization (especially when most of the unseen workers who make them in factories in the developing world are women), and they don't offer liberation from the male gaze or any other substantial freedom. That gear for sale, however, gives the women who can afford it opportunities to move their bodies in new ways and to invent personae to present the world. It's a shame there always has to be someone watching.

I haven't really taken advantage of the spectacular gear market—I'm not indifferent to fashion generally, but to running fashion specifically. It still seems very strange to me that I can convince people I'm a certain kind of runner just by wearing the right clothes. My sneakers and tights are comfortable, but I don't wear them to shop for groceries or to meet a friend for coffee.

Accordingly, my running wardrobe is pretty nondescript. It's getting increasingly faded, it's not sexy, and it's an even bet as to whether a given item will be clean or not when I put it on. I own several pairs of shorts (black, blue, green, gray) and several synthetic singlets (purple, pink, black, yellow, gray, orange) and a few pairs of stretchy tights. The garments that once were bright have had their zing washed out. None of my singlets have motivational slogans printed on them, although sometimes I run in an old, grubby women's collective T-shirt, hand-printed in the 1990s with that peerless feminist mantra RIOTS NOT DIETS. That usually gets a second look when I'm running laps of the park. (I wish I still had the one with a little girl in plaits and a flouncy dress holding a sparking bomb beneath the slogan BOMB THE PATRIARCHY.) I have a new pair of sneakers and an old pair of sneakers that I upgrade when the padding behind the heels wears through. If it's very cold, I wear black and gray compression tights, but I'm certain they don't make me run faster. I've worked through many pairs of fashion crisis no-name sunglasses with polarized lenses that block at least some light coming in from the sides. All in all, it's not so much a triumph of careful self-presentation as a lazy effort to avoid making an impression.

*

When those Paris shopgirls, the midinettes, first ran their race in 1903, they dressed as if for a picnic. A large illustration that appeared in a weekly newspaper, *Le Petit Journal*, shows the midinettes at the starting line. Loose blouses are neatly tucked into long skirts that swish gracefully beneath their knees. All the midinettes are running in stockings and boots buttoned at the side. Some have adorned their blouses with fancy lace yokes; others have tied big floppy bows around their necks. Every head carries a hat: berets, smart short-brimmed straw hats, fancier felt hats with ribbons. The only hint that this is a sporting event is that all the runners have a pale blue armband with a number printed on it.

Two gendarmes watch from horseback, along with a big crowd of men on the sidelines, a few of whom are holding their

hats in the air in encouragement. The winner, Jeanne Chemi-
nel, finished in seventy minutes. *Le Petit Journal* records that
she was "*une agréable brune*" (a pleasant-looking brunette), but
didn't ask her why she'd entered the race. For those who didn't
get to ogle the beauties on the day, postcards featuring buxom
shopgirls in running poses made the rounds in Paris after the
race.

The midinettes were working women with modest incomes
of their own. Their livelihoods were tied up with the production of desirable, fashionable items for sale. Journalists treated
these runners as goods on display, but I'm curious about what
lies beyond the illustrations. What were they chatting about as
they waited to start? It would surely be anachronistic to script
a set of girl power slogans for them. Maybe they were worried
about whether they'd be able to run the distance. Did they wish
they could hitch up their skirts and roll up their sleeves, even
if that meant exposing their calves and lower arms? Maybe
they were pressing their leather boots against their heels and
making blister predictions. Maybe they were giggling to themselves about all the pervy guys on the sidelines as they eyed off
potential suitors.

A few decades later, when Violet Piercy ran to establish
that her marathon record really *was* hers, the dress code had
evolved somewhat—although she's still attired as if for a day
out. In 1927, on the Pathé newsreel I mentioned earlier, Piercy
ran in black shorts and a collared white jumper. It's made of
heavy cloth, onto which the crest of a sporting club has been
patched. Her appearance has been thoroughly de-eroticized,
and it seems to me that her male chaperones are there to warn

cinema audiences against seeing her as eye candy. On her feet are what look like Mary Janes strapped over little white socks. The shoes have short heels, and her legs are otherwise bare. I can't imagine how she ran a marathon in them. She has a cute bob and wears a wool hat that could be mistaken for a cloche. Her appearance is nothing like what I would have expected. Shorts are the only garment that she and I have in common. She looks like an overgrown schoolgirl on her way to an art school party, not an athlete.

The athletic women who appear in Leni Riefenstahl's 1935 propaganda film *Triumph of the Will* embody a more recognizable female athleticism. They are wholesome and strong, and their functional clothing does not impede their movements. Such images define a certain kind of idealized, muscular femininity, one built on conformity, hard work, and obedience. In the 1936 Berlin Olympic Games, there were no distance running events for women, but women wore much less restrictive uniforms to compete in swimming, shorter track events, and field sports. What would a few decades earlier have seemed distressingly immodest and unladylike was becoming accepted, and so too was the idea of female athleticism.

And yet, for all these developments, as we've seen, women runners still looked like trouble to many people, especially sports officials: women who would willfully imperil their capacity to bear children; women who didn't care how they looked. Trouble. Not only were the female distance athletes who broke through in the late 1960s and early '70s challenging ideas about how far a woman's body could run, but they were also rewriting the rules about what women runners look like, effectively challenging centuries of visual history. It took a few decades for clothing manufacturers to catch up with them and provide women who run with extensive, expensive choices.

*

Every so often when people discover that I like to run, they look me up and down, as if sizing up a racehorse, and tell me that I look like a runner. The hint of a claim that I might be some kind of athlete is taken to make my body available for inspection. I find it all terribly uncomfortable. Perhaps novice male runners are also subject to such assessments, but it seems to me that there's something irrevocably gendered about this gaze.

What does it mean to tell a woman that she looks like a runner? The standard image of the female distance runner: long-legged, with narrow hips and shoulders, small breasts, and low body fat. This is the most efficient physiology in terms of gait and load; of course, many spectacular runners shaped very differently have won medals and broken records. Kathrine Switzer, for example, is very tall. In terms of height, I am decidedly middle-sized. My shoulders are not very broad, but my hips are, which cancels out any advantage my longish legs might bring. I've always carried enough body fat to keep me from gauntness, and I wouldn't think of running without a sports bra. When it comes down to it, I don't look much like a runner at all. That's just what people say to account for staring at me in such a clinical and invasive manner.

Usually it's the low-body-fat part of looking like a runner that gets my interlocutors interested. That running is an extremely effective way to burn calories is touted as one of its great benefits. And so, when I'm told that I look like a runner, I wait for the questions about weight loss to come. Did I start running to change my appearance? (No.) Did I go on a diet? (No.) Do I have any weight-loss tips? (No.) How much weight did I lose? (Gah.) What is it that puts my body up for grabs like this? After a few years, I got fed up with being looked at and sick of the questions. I used to explain that my discovery of what my body could do was much more interesting than anything about body fat, but now I rarely bother.

The last time I ran the City2Surf, I saw a pair of women in matching T-shirts scrawled with bare breasts and hands groping them. Is that what a woman runner looks like? It made me laugh out loud because it's such a crude rejoinder to all these anxieties about women running. That image out–Benny Hilled Benny Hill; it administered an excellent up-yours to the sleaze brigade. I haven't gone out and bought a T-shirt like this, and I haven't shed my desire to be invisible. I don't want to be a sideshow; I don't want anyone to mistake the glee, exhaustion and indifference I might display when running for fear. When I most enjoy running, my limbs swing through the air as if heavy weights have been untethered from them. That's when it stops feeling like a performance and, finally, it's all movement.

8

REJOICE, WE CONQUER!

I kept running and, gradually, it became a habit. I ran another half marathon, and then another and another. My race times weren't impressive, but I'd learned how to move. I could run just like anybody else. Any residual concerns about the awkwardness of my scratched knees and flapping elbows drifted away. If I was tired, I simply slowed down, and sometimes I walked.

Old certainties gave way to new ones. I knew how fit I needed to be to run 13 miles. First, work up to running 6 miles, then nudge a little farther each week. If I could run 11 miles in training, I would be able to run a half marathon on race day. I couldn't spell out such equations to myself without chuckling. *Race day.* I knew that if, after a training run or race, I didn't stretch the big muscles that strap around the femur, my gait would be stiff the next day. I knew what sort of push I needed in my legs and lungs to run up a hill; that if my hips started to grate, I could keep running, but that if I landed hard after leaping off a gutter and jarred my knee, I'd have to walk home. I could predict the furious hunger that kicked in an hour or so after a long run, and the deep weariness that would take me to bed in the evening.

Hitherto I'd been unable to understand feedback mechanisms that govern the body. After Mum and Dad died, I was always tired but rarely able to sleep the night through. Sometimes I ate for comfort; often my view of hunger and satiety was clouded by emotion. Now, I observed closely the relationship between exertion and sleep from week to week. An icy bright negroni, even early in the evening, would turn my feet to lead the following morning. Pasta was top-notch running fuel; potato chips were not. A salad was always too little; lasagna was always too much. In no other areas of my life were the dividends on behavior so simple to calculate. There was a balance to this empiricism that pleased me enormously. I became aware that I was both healthy and mobile, and very lucky to be so—that I might one day not be able to run, due to sickness or injury, was a grim thought. I had no children competing for my attention in the mornings, and my work schedule was flexible enough to accommodate both running and recovery. As I logged more half marathons, I could see no compelling reason why I could not run even farther.

Thirteen miles is a substantial distance, but it's only half a marathon. Running a marathon had once seemed to me as abstract a goal as swimming to the horizon from the beach. An idea that I'd used as a trampoline, springing higher and higher until I could see what was over the fence next door, and then past the garden beyond. If I could jump high enough to gain a clear view of the neighborhood, I could run a marathon. If I could run a marathon, I could cartwheel into the future, brightly colored ribbons twirling from my wrists and ankles. I would relinquish this jerky, bouncing fantasy of transcendence in favor of the movement registered by the swishing reflective strips on my shoes, the rhythm picked out by my knees and my elbows.

When I talked about running to my friends, I told them with great confidence that I'd run a marathon, one day. I'd applied very little thought, however, to how I might actually prepare to run a marathon, or when that one day might fall. A blast of January resolve finally prompted me to confront the question, *When will I run a marathon?* The answer turned out to be: *This year!* I picked a spring marathon in Sydney and gave myself lots of time to train, many more months than I needed. With caution, I sketched the outlines of a training program, the beginning of another beginning. I bought a book about running a first marathon and egged myself on by reading lurid testimonials about running the distance, even though their sentimentality made me squirm: *My proudest achievement*; *A complete personal revolution*; *Don't ever believe you can't do it.*

Many ancient traditions of thought applaud the cultivation of the body as a virtue. The Greeks called it *arete*. Training for a marathon, however, far exceeds the requirements of living a balanced life, of being a good sport, of shaking out the mental cobwebs. There are less risky ways to get very fit, and certainly many that are less time-consuming. Just running regularly would do the trick. Joining a sports team is much more convivial. Marathons aren't the best path to weight loss, stress relief, greater energy—and to train for one involves courting the risk of serious joint injury. I heard anecdotes about scores of other people's uncles and cousins who had blown their knees on the marathon circuit. And yet, I let the marathon in my mind glisten with the promise that it would yield extraordinary benefits, benefits that would outflank the perils and discomfort of training.

Even atheists like me, who can't curl up in the embrace of a benevolent fatality, clutch at marathon magic. It's easy to get carried away by it all, and I certainly did. The finish line I endowed with the qualities of an enchanted threshold: if I could cross that line, I would stumble, transformed, into a new realm. Could my legs carry me that far, and if so, what then? In this vision the marathon became a kind of feminist fairy tale, in which damsels in distress rediscover themselves as conquering queens.

These were returns that a simple regimen of weekend running couldn't deliver. I would finally articulate with my body the stories about grief and recovery that I had been unable to put into words. I entertained a secret hope: something in me that had been knocked out of place when my parents died might be knocked back into place. What a strange and still-desperate manifestation of optimism that was, although I didn't recognize this then.

*

Like the glitter that sparkles on so many lucky charms, the glamour of the marathon is only superficial. It's run over a distance just a bit farther than the 25-odd miles separating the

Greek town of Marathon from Athens. It's based on an almost certainly inaccurate measurement of the distance between these two points, and a historically shaky account of events that may have taken place two and a half thousand years ago. It's certainly not an ancient test of self.

To the men who founded the marathon, the long run was a means of telling a story about the endurance of ancient virtues in the modern world. The first marathon was run in 1896 and until midway through the twentieth century marathons attracted only tiny fields of runners. The wide uptake of the marathon as an exercise in self-definition—one that even so-so athletes such as myself might consider—dates to the 1960s, not exactly the dawn of time.

In 1894, as bureaucrats and aristocrats chewed over the details of the first modern Olympic Games, a French philologist, Michel Bréal, hit on the idea of a footrace called a marathon to honor Pheidippides, one of the great messenger-runners of the ancient world. It would be run from the Plain of Marathon to the Pnyx of Athens. Bréal offered a handsome silver cup as a prize. The proposal was greeted with gusto, and when the young Greek runner Spyridon Louis won the event, he was hailed as a hero running in the footsteps of the ancients. The silver cup is now on display at the Acropolis Museum in Athens, an irregular exhibit in a building otherwise dedicated to marbles sculpted over two thousand years ago.

There had been several halfhearted attempts to revive the ancient Olympic Games in the nineteenth century, but Pierre de Coubertin, patriarch of the modern Olympic movement, applied himself to the task with formidable energy. The fourth son of French royalist aristocrats, de Coubertin established the International Olympic Committee in 1894. He persuaded bureaucrats and wealthy benefactors that the Games were a matter of nothing less than world peace. Sports for the greater good—and an opportunity to quash widely held concerns that too much civilized living was turning white men into degenerate weaklings. Women and nonwhite men fell beyond the reckoning of the architects of the Games, as if their degeneracy was a foregone conclusion.

The motto of the Olympic movement—*citius, altius, fortius*; faster, higher, stronger—was de Coubertin's work, and his exhaustingly long writings on sports are crammed with variations on the same theme: the worthiness of hierarchies based on strength and speed. In one volume, as he recalls a visit to the public schools of England, de Coubertin writes approvingly that "the muscles are made to do the work of a moral educationer." As a hopeless schoolgirl athlete, I had languished at the slow and weak end of de Coubertin's natural order. I'd since picked up some lessons that might have pleased him: exertion can be its own reward; persistence can yield improvement. And yet, I'd also come to much happier terms with my limitations as an athlete. An ethos of curiosity rather than competition had guided my running practice, and no one was going to give me a medal for that.

De Coubertin died in 1937, having spent his fortune promoting the International Olympic Committee; in a final touch of pageantry, he requested that his heart be buried in Olympus. Without him, it's unlikely either that the Games would have been reestablished or that the marathon would have come into existence. Perhaps if Michel Bréal had raised the idea of a long-distance footrace in some other forum—but who can

say if it would have stirred the same sentiments without the
carnival of the Games and de Coubertin's persuasive powers.

*

De Coubertin was hardly alone in seeking to connect a flour-
ishing contemporary Europe to the achievements of classical
Greece. There was great enthusiasm for the ancient world in
late nineteenth-century Europe and the feats of antiquity were
alive in the popular imagination. Excavations in Greece—including at Olympia—and Egypt had brought plundered statues
into the museums of the continent's great capitals. Avatars of
unforgotten civilizations, these became touchstones for poets
and statesmen alike, who framed the magnificent present as
a deserving successor to that grand past. Why, then, as this
Hellenism thrived, was Pheidippides the model for the long-
distance athlete, and not one of the many other great runners
of the Greek world, such as fleet-footed Achilles or Atalanta?

Pheidippides was a runner-messenger who loped between
Athens, Sparta, and Marathon at the behest of the Athenian
leaders during the Battle of Marathon. At first blush, it may
seem strange that the aristocrats who conceived of the modern
Olympics celebrated a humble runner, not a general, a states-
man, or a god—but their decision points to the significance of
the Battle of Marathon to nineteenth-century understandings
of the glorious continuity of Western civilization. It's the kind
of East versus West narrative to which conservative historians
inevitably return.

The inhabitants of democratic Athens had fearfully awaited

the attack of the mighty Persian navy, led by the tyrant Darius. Against all expectations, Athens prevailed: the city won the Battle of Marathon and eventually the Persian Wars. Athens victorious, democracy also prevailed. In 1828, John Stuart Mill appraised the conflict, which took place in 490 BCE:

> The battle of Marathon, even as an event in English history, is more important than the battle of Hastings. If the issue of that day had been different, the Britons and the Saxons might still have been wandering in the woods.

The achievement of Pheidippides as a runner is the centerpiece of marathon mythology: a symbolic celebration of the triumph of the democratic tradition. In these few, quick rhetorical moves, the marathon was thus established as an event that took in the epic sweep of Western history. If marathon runners seem self-absorbed, self-important, the Battle of Marathon can be invoked to make their efforts sound tremendously worthwhile. Can volleyball matches or strength-training classes claim this kind of lineage?

It wasn't all a matter of politics. The reputation of the runner of Marathon had received a boost when Robert Browning's poem "Pheidippides" was published in 1879. A dramatic monologue on endurance, this literary hit primed the imaginations of English and American readers for the 1896 marathon. Browning's messenger ran more than 300 miles in just a few days—more than ten marathons. This runner was a "noble strong man," a man "who could race like a god, bear the face of a god, whom a god loved so well." For all that, he is flesh and blood, unable to transcend his mortality. Pheidippides collapses, ecstatic, when his message is delivered:

"Rejoice, we conquer!" Like wine thro' clay,
Joy in his blood bursting his heart, he died—the bliss!

And thus it ends for Browning's messenger, in a fatal cardiac explosion of joy. His bliss is an extreme case of runners' high, the post-exertion euphoria chased by so many distance junkies.

Browning's lines on the death of Pheidippides are widely quoted in motivational books about running, which has always struck me as an odd form of encouragement. That fist-pumping iamb, the injunction to "Rejoice" and the skittering exultation of the dactyl—"we conquer!"—are a stirring combination, but their effect is diminished by the immediate death of the runner. Of the blissfulness, I'm not convinced. The glory of Pheidippides's death reads to me like just another version of *dulce et decorum est*. How sweet and noble is it to run yourself to death? How's an amateur runner to emulate *that* commitment?

Mortal and menial though Pheidippides may have been, only a very few super-fit ultramarathon runners would be able to cover the hundreds of miles that Browning attributes to him. In 2010, roughly two and a half thousand years after the Battle of Marathon, a Greek runner, Maria Polyzou, ran from Athens to Sparta and back. She was part of a group of runners who attempted this distance. It's pleasing to me that the only one of this cohort who actually made it was a woman. For most runners, achieving such a feat is as remote as one of the labors of Heracles. The decision of the organizers of the

1896 Olympic Games to restrict their marathon to the distance between Marathon and Athens bequeathed us an event that's extremely challenging but not impossible. The training guides promise that anyone can run a marathon, hastily advising beginners to see a doctor first. Maybe they were right, but before I started running, a marathon might as well have been a thousand miles.

The sources collated by Browning, and by Bréal, present variations on the story of Pheidippides, but all agree that a runner was involved in the Battle of Marathon. The distractible, chatty Herodotus offers the only near-contemporary account in his *Histories*, written sixty years after the Persian Wars. Herodotus's messenger is named Philippides; we're told only that he runs from Athens to Sparta. (Browning makes the poor guy run back to Athens, to Marathon, and then back to Athens again.) Pliny the Elder, Plutarch, and Lucian—historians born at least five hundred years later, after the birth of Christ—each tell slightly different versions. As in all good running yarns, the details are dwarfed by the great significance of the run itself. After all, who will be able to contest the details of my running stories? If my nieces get excited about my first races and decide to tell their kids about them, what will be distorted in the telling?

Browning drew a little on all the ancient sources to give flesh and form to Pheidippides—and then filled in the rest himself. His messenger is a contemporary athlete who prefigures de Coubertin's vision of the committed athlete. Browning's Pheidippides isn't just a man doing his job; there's no question that he'll give up or rest. He gives his all—and his exertions save democracy. He's the cricketer doing it for Australia, the baseball player doing his hometown proud—the athlete whose sport has been elevated to a civic duty. Those who run in Pheidippides's footsteps are participating in a ritualized celebration of the democratic tradition. (This was also true of the first Boston Marathon, which was run on April 19, 1897, Patriots' Day: a holiday that commemorates the run of another wartime messenger, Paul Revere.)

Well, that's the official story. The marathon celebrates the kind of democracy in which messengers like Pheidippides and working men like Spyridon Louis knew their place. When the first Olympic Games were held, the Great Game of European diplomatic rivalries was intensifying. That culminated in the First World War and the slaughter of millions of young men from the countries who'd sent athletes to compete in 1896. The grand democratic tradition hadn't granted a vote to women in most parts of the world by 1896—and women, of course, weren't welcomed as participants in the ancient games at Olympus or the first modern Games. The legend that's been cobbled together to serve the marathon is a boy's adventure about the meaning of male sacrifice in war. If it's part of an ancient tradition, it's one that involves men telling stories to each other and ignoring women.

Why had I been so captivated by all this? Running a marathon is still a sign of socioeconomic status: people like me, with time and leisure and culturally formed aspirations, choose to run marathons and then blather on about them at tedious dinner parties. I can't remember when I first heard about marathons; I suspect it was when I was eight or nine years old and my father was hurling himself into endurance sports. I learned then what a triathlon is, and I must have picked up on some triumphal rhetoric about marathons. I don't remember my mother being anything other than supportive of my father's training, though she obviously wasn't moved to run a marathon herself. Or maybe she was—but all her time was occupied by her four small children.

When I studied ancient history in high school, I loved reading Herodotus and Thucydides, and marveled that I could encounter their worlds through literature. When I first saw the Parthenon Marbles in the British Museum, my impulse was to touch them and connect myself to all the centuries they'd endured. Later, when I understood that they were stolen, my understanding of that endurance shifted. A similar instinct to attach myself to an epic continuity of human endeavor first drew me to the marathon—but I told myself that if I ever actually managed to run one, I wouldn't be celebrating war. If I was going to run 26 miles, I'd take Browning's lead and refashion the story for my own purposes. I'd run against patriarchal history and, eternal virtues of strength and speed be damned, I'd run as slowly as I liked.

*

There was no way I'd be able to tough out a marathon on a wave of determination and raw talent. I had no raw talent, and I'd needed more than determination to run half marathons. Rather than a one-off test of strength, I resigned myself to a long period of training. Self-discipline, tenacity, muscles, confidence: I'd pack it all into my apprenticeship. It would be tough—in moments like these, I addressed myself in the assured basso that I'd heard football coaches use on TV—but I'd faced tougher stuff. *Can I do it? I can do it!* I would move in an orderly fashion through each stage of training, from exertion to recovery. I shrugged at the likelihood of inconvenience and fatigue—surely I'd endured greater impositions on my days than long runs.

I've met runners who jog for pleasure and never enter events, but they're the exception: to most of the runners I encounter, the structure offered by training for a race seems to be almost as significant as the activity itself. It's my guess that the structure of training programs is what leads so many avowed nonrunners to attempt marathons when their lives fall apart. For every sports-crazy glycogen junkie at the starting line, there's someone who is recently divorced, whose child has died, who has survived chemotherapy, who's found herself shocked, bereft, and still somehow alive. *Enduring* and *coping* are synonyms, and the logic seems to go something like this: *If my body can endure a marathon, then my soul, my psyche, whatever it is that comprises my* self, *can blunder on too.* This is a different motivation than the distress that compels the literary runners I'd met. The aftermath of loss is exhausting, repetitious, and often very, very dull—and so is training for a marathon. But endurance can help turn elusive sorrows into something tangible, like aching muscles and blisters. Such pains can be easily described, unlike the pain of grief. Online forums for beginner marathoners are overflowing with anonymous stories about recovery written by those who've found some solace from chaos and dread.

I didn't recognize myself in the full-throttle sports books or even the unbearably upbeat guides for beginners. *I'm nothing like those people*, I grumbled to myself. And yet I flittered closer to catch glimpses of experiences that I might recognize, tantalized by the prospect of insight. The theory that, in extremis, we may be able to access our true and possibly best selves at our breaking points has many precedents. That suffering will yield truth is the stuff of tragedy; follow the muse Melpomene: after catharsis, order.

What if these themes preoccupied the megaphone-holding men at the beginning of distance events? What if, instead of asking, *Who's feeling frisky?*, they asked, *Who's had a terrible year? Who's struggled to connect to the world? Who hopes that this run will shake it all back into place?* There would be shrugs, and friends would exchange baffled glances. Maybe a few people would find that a painful, awkward sob had been dredged up. I'm so jumpy and defensive at the starting line that I'd probably roll my eyes and mutter something about how this had turned into a two-bit self-help forum. *Get on with it.*

The truth is, I wonder about the people who cheer frantically when megaphones turn to personal bests and the pain barrier. If they were seated Encounter-group style and asked, again and again, *Why are you here? Why are you really here?* what would they answer? I'd expect versions of familiar formulae: *I wanted to see if I could do it. I wanted to test myself. I just thought it was time for a change. I'm getting older.* I'd listen closely, encourage them to keep talking; I'd wait to hear them say the same things over and over again. And finally the themes would emerge in their raw form: mortality, pain, and the terrifying unknowability of the body's limits.

One friend, a literary scholar, surprised me when I told her I was going to run a marathon. She just nodded sagely. "This sounds like you," she said. "You battled through a PhD and you've read all the big modernists. You're used to endurance. You'll be fine." I turned her implacable encouragement into something like a motto: I'd read all the big modernists, I could run a marathon. Roger, a family friend and veteran marathoner, was generous with his counsel too. He told me that the couple of long meditation retreats I'd endured in my twenties would help much more than any time in the gym—I already had an insight into the state of mind I'd need to commit to the training.

Many friends looked faintly worried, however, when I told them what I was planning to do. Maybe they sensed the hint of drama in the air; maybe they withheld their flickering suspicions that a current of self-destructive behavior had only just been averted. A half marathon sounds like a far more moderate affair. *Are you sure you're up to it?* I was asked. *That's a terribly long way. Don't you think something more* manageable *would be appropriate? Manageable*, I'd reply. *What's manageable?* I stopped trying to decipher the concerns coded in these questions and presented a defiant, slightly flippant demeanor. *Who do you think I am—a junior analyst up for a performance review?* I assured them that if I trained carefully, I would be able to make the distance. *Don't worry, I'm not out to break any records.* That became my standard line.

*

The half marathon that I've run most frequently knots around the center of Sydney each May. It starts and ends in Hyde Park, not too far from the apartment building in which I lived for a decade. The route changes only a little each year. The planners have to negotiate Sydney's perennial clog of roadworks and building projects to come up with a course that delivers some big money harbor views, that isn't too hilly, that doesn't throw the Sunday morning traffic to shit, and that has a few nice straights. No doubt various athletic organizations impose their own requirements. What it means in practice is a course with a few curly loops and awkward hairpin bends, and some surprising route-enabling connections up and down overpass ramps and along tight one-way streets. A strange mix of glorious Sydney and nondescript inner-city concrete, the harbor on one side, the backs of parking lots and service roads on the other.

The principles behind training for a marathon aren't fundamentally different from those that guide half marathoners: a weekly long run that becomes progressively longer anchors the training program, and shorter, faster weekday runs fill it out. By now I was very familiar with the 13 miles of a half marathon. I had learned how to slow down in the first half so that I would not have to walk the second. I knew that the first 3 or 4 miles are almost effortless, and that a terrible boredom can kick in after 8 or 9. I tried to train myself not to notice the mile markers in the middle of the event, hoping that I would surprise myself and find that I had only 3 miles left to run and not 4 or 5. I learned how to calculate my pace using my watch and the kilometer markers, with the goal of moving at the same speed for the entire race. I came to terms with frustratingly irregular experiences of distance: 3 miles from the finish line feels fantastically farther than 2 miles. I'd already learned so much. I thought all I'd need to do would be find the time to run more.

A tiny network of runners developed among my circles of friends. A couple of women I had known for years started to run, and we exchanged training tales, surprised by a new intimacy. They didn't approach the sport in the way that I did, solo and slowly; they joined groups and trained with greater commitment than me. I always ran alone, but I'd nod and wave when I passed other runners in the morning. If distant friends and acquaintances posted pictures of their running triumphs on social media, I browsed them with bemused recognition. Every now and then, I posted my own photos, advertising that I too had become a runner.

I was working as an editor in a small, open-plan office, and two colleagues were marathon runners. Whenever our publishing schedule slowed, they gave me training advice and answered my many questions. Was it okay to have skipped a weekday run? Did I really have to run intervals? And I discovered runners from my past: a former roommate who'd played video games until dawn was now doing half marathons; a researcher whom I'd got to know smoking outside libraries had turned over a new leaf and planned to run a marathon; a stockbroker friend took a "career break" to train for an iron-man. Neighbors appeared in the fruit shop line wearing marathon T-shirts; baristas wore marathon visors; the ex-lovers of old friends turned up at half marathons; one-time cocktail companions went home early to prepare for morning runs.

My indefatigable cousins were also running half marathons regularly, and so were their partners and half-siblings and partner's cousins and college friends. My sisters sensibly left us to it. Each year, a larger family group would congregate in the starting area of the big Sydney half marathons. Thanks to an uneven distribution of athleticism across the family, my cousins would always finish long before I did. The upside was a cheering squad waiting for me when I crossed the line.

*

Racing—though that still seems like an overblown term for the events I've completed—is very different than training. For me, it is in the everydayness of training that the pleasure of running lies. Cognitive behavioral therapists and Protestant guides to self-improvement are fixated on good habits, especially when they can be aligned with larger changes in well-being. If a habit becomes second nature, then, so the thinking goes, we face fewer stressful decisions and can live a little more lightly.

A good running habit should involve an alarm and a burst of energy, without a moment of indecision to separate them. I've known and chucked several ostensibly bad habits: smoking cigarettes, staying home in bed, letting the phone ring out, pessimism, crappy television, crappy novels. Procrastination might be understood as the purgatory between good and bad habits, and I've spent time there too. The usual objection to habits is that they make life routine, that the burden of self-coercion dulls spontaneity. This didn't worry me. I had lived for a long time without much of a structure of self-care. Having my runs as a steady, predictable element of my week was preferable to the survival-mode reactivity—the less glossy version of spontaneity—that had governed so much of my adult life.

I didn't reorganize my life around my running schedule; I've never quite pulled that off. I slotted in weekday runs where

I could and saved my habit-forming energies for a weekend splurge on a long run. As Freud and everyone else knows, there's pleasure in repetition, and the habits I built around my long runs were evidence of this principle.

I would get up as early as I could and go straight to the kitchen for a hasty breakfast. I'd smear honey and peanut butter on a slice of nubbly toast and eat it, still standing, as I watched the sky change color through the kitchen window. Then, a little banana, a big glass of water, a tiny espresso: the order of these mornings became a ritual. I'd start to run exactly an hour after finishing my coffee. I had time to get dressed, to make sure my shoes were exactly tied, to rub sunscreen over my face and shoulders. In my pocket I'd stuff a $20 bill, insurance against old fears that I might not be able to get home under my own steam. If I didn't need a bus or a taxi—and I never did—I'd buy a sugary drink and gulp it down as I walked the last leg home. If I planned to run farther than 10 miles, I'd take a sachet of one of those revolting sweet carbohydrate gels or some jelly beans with me too. It's fuel, I'd tell myself, as if I were an expert in biochemistry.

I was drawn to the same spots each weekend. I loved running around the tip of Mrs. Macquaries Point, with Woolloomooloo and the big gray ships of Garden Island on one side, and the great open harbor on the other. Along the sandstone-edged paths in the Botanical Gardens I'd pass Bronwyn Oliver's melancholy sculptures of oversized pods—still, I think, my favorite artworks in the city. Heavy fallen bronzes, it is as if they rolled to the water's edge from an ancient tree and stayed as a reminder of the life and fecundity of the site before the bridges and parks and roads were built.

Brilliant postcard views: from Kirribilli, the Harbour Bridge rising from its magnificent and lonely northern pylon; from the Aquarium, Luna Park smirking beneath the firmament marked by the Bridge; looking eastward from the highest pitch of the Bridge, out over the brash, rhinestone-speckled water to the Opera House and washed-out little Pinchgut. Blazing skies, stormy skies. A friend who'd decamped to London told me he'd left because Sydney was so beautiful that it made us all lazy, killed our ambitions. Only when I started to run did I understand the addictive pull of the harbor and grasp its connection to the horrors of property prices. In the early morning on the Bridge there are dog walkers, jet-lagged tourists, harried parents pushing babies in strollers, lots of runners, brunching couples, and many amateur photographers. Even on dank days, the water is bright. Sunglasses, lattes, aggression: the Sydney clichés proliferate as you cross the Bridge. Faced with that eternal harbor, who cares?

To be a runner is to enjoy a sensibility attuned to place— light and shadow, gradient, the surfaces that move underfoot—and to be largely indifferent to real estate, an unusual vantage point in Sydney. As I ran, high fences striped me with shadows in the morning sun. I sought out the wooden decking at Cockle Bay Wharf and Darling Harbour, and congratulated myself on giving my knees a break from the concrete. I looked out to see the algal stains on the wharves and piers when the tide was low, and when it was high, to watch the water splash up onto the jetties. Water everywhere: seeping through sandstone, motionless in swimming pools, billowing after ferries, breaking new paths from the inland to the harbor. Rushes of honeysuckle, frangipani, and orange blossom in Lavender Bay.

The frustratingly uneven pavement on the steep climb up from McMahons Point. Shafts of light breaking through the tangled branches of giant figs. I used to run through Millers Point and down to the shore of Barangaroo, along a deep flank of the harbor that was shut off to pedestrians for years. Now there's a new park there, and a casino half built, and I can remember what it was like before all the development, when the view west to that stretch of water was still being wrangled over by politicians. My body carries a record of the city's history, my version of it, anyway.

I knew that when I arrived home, I would hunger for oranges, so I tried to make sure that there would be at least one waiting for me in my fruit bowl. I got my act together to have clean shorts and socks ready for the weekends; I ate a proper dinner and went to bed early the night before my long runs. Buying oranges and getting my laundry done: I wasn't exactly following Pheidippides, out there delivering messages and dying for the state. Instead, in the name of running a marathon, I began to take care of myself a little better.

Often I'd meet my sister Laura after these runs, and together we'd cross the city to have lunch with our grandfather. Claudia and Lucy had moved out of Sydney years earlier, but if they were in town they would join us too. Each time I'd make the same salad with ingredients that had been decided by consensus years earlier: iceberg lettuce, a short lecture on the pitfalls of modern greens from my grandfather, shallots, avocado, Dijon mustard vinaigrette, and verification by Laura that it didn't contain cucumber. My grandfather would pour us each a glass of the same sauvignon blanc he poured every week, which he'd taste before declaring his preference for beer. We would sit in the same configuration of chairs on his balcony. That night, I would sleep soundly.

I let myself become fixated on the marathon and its parameters. What proportion of the distance had I run? How long would it take me to run 26 miles at this pace? My email address had been added to several running enthusiast mailing lists—I'd failed to check the "don't contact me" box on entering races. I didn't unsubscribe right away, letting my inbox instead clog with ads for new gear. I was a runner. The marketing departments of Nike and ASICS recognized me as such, even though I didn't upgrade my shoes or buy a GPS watch or a belt on which to strap fuel bottles. Eventually, I'd delete these emails, but I did it with a grin on my face at finding myself an inhabitant of this new category.

I noticed that if I didn't run every couple of days, I became edgy. My appetite changed, and so did my sleeping patterns. I became used to the strange shifts of emotional energy that take place over the course of a long run. Suppressed rages and distress would pound at my temples, and then disappear. I'd be muttering to myself about something or someone, and then a black cocker spaniel would distract me, the traffic lights would change, I'd turn a new corner and find an easy downhill stretch ahead of me. I listened for the beat of my footsteps on the pavement, but usually they were lost in the hum of the city. A state of constant, steady movement was my aspiration. If you try to rush when running long distances, you run out of steam. If you run too slowly, you never get home. Marathon runners are supposed to include sprints and faster tempo runs in their training, but I found the changes in pace too tumultuous. I wanted only to run for a long time, and to be soothed by the incomprehensible emotional shifts this produced.

The marathon had a hold on me—but I didn't always manage to stick to my training program. It is, I discovered, exhausting to train for a marathon. It was more difficult than I had anticipated to fit life around 30 or 40 miles of running a week. The distance puts a strain on the heart, the joints, and the muscles. Most of the time, I didn't worry about whether I was refashioning patriarchal history or not. I was just too tired.

9

PLAN B

I ran and I ran but I didn't finish that first marathon. I didn't
finish it because I didn't start it. I'd filled in the forms with
so much merriment, relishing the prospect of a long run with a
beginning, a middle, and an end. I would run a marathon and
watch the world change. So I ran and I ran and I grew much
stronger, but as the date of the big race drew closer, I realized I
didn't have a hope of running my way to a triumphant conclusion. I simply wasn't fit enough. The toll of sheer fatigue was
too high. This was no pathetic capitulation to self-doubt. It was
an objective assessment of my fitness. I had left too many holes
in my training program unpatched. No amount of self-belief
and positive thinking would have carried me 26 miles, and I
doubted I'd be ready to run 20. So I filled out a change-of-entry
form and faxed it to the event organizers in time for the cut-off
date. The woman at the post office wanted to talk running, but

I didn't and I left, mumbling my apologies. A few weeks later, I ran a gloomy half marathon.

What had happened? As joyful as my long runs had been, they just hadn't been long enough, and I'd skipped too many weekday sessions. I babbled on about running whenever I could, but training wasn't the sole focus of my weeks. As the year wore on, my grandfather had become unwell, and I'd spent many evenings with him, drinking remedial whisky and bickering over the news; I wouldn't necessarily rise early the next day to go running. It had been a rainy winter, and I'd tucked myself into the corner of a couch and rewatched several seasons of *The West Wing*. Those late nights cost me a few runs too. I wrecked myself on a back-country ski trip, lugging a heavy pack in sleety weather and sleeping in the snow. I returned home bone-weary, and weeks passed before I could run as far or as fast as I had before I left.

In a fit of enthusiasm, I'd joined a running group that met in Centennial Park, but only turned up to one session. I ran close to last in a 5-kilometer time trial, and the long-term members of the group didn't speak to me. "Typical stupid unfriendly bully jocks," I muttered on the way home. I could see myself being yanked back into the past, to a school playground where I was slow and clumsy. I struggled to view this lightly, as just another encounter with contingency and not as a sign of grotesque personal lack. Maybe if I'd stuck with the running group and toughed out the lukewarm welcome, I would have found some discipline. The group might have generated sufficient fear of humiliation to motivate me.

I was irritated with myself, of course, and worried that dropping out of the marathon meant I'd reached my limit.

Maybe half marathons were all I could manage. One runner friend told me that I'd had too long to train. "Next time, give yourself less preparation time," he counseled, "and then you'll feel that every run is urgent."

If marathons are supposed to make you feel like a million bucks, opting out is a monumental downer. If the marathon is a yardstick that can be used to measure achievement, it can also measure failure. Was there a lesson that I was supposed to learn from this defeat? I already knew I wasn't a natural athlete and that I'd need to train carefully to succeed. Was I just too lazy? What was the appropriate response to this situation? *Control your impulses! Defeat the weakness! Find the time! No excuses!* I did what I could to shove away the impulse to bullying self-reproach.

A plodding few months followed in which I didn't run quite so frequently. Tired and disappointed, I felt the strength sap out of my muscles as I idealized my former super-fit state. Why was I able to get up in the morning then and go running? Who was that diligent person who wouldn't drink more than two glasses of wine the night before a biggish run? I joked my way through a little clown act about how one day I'd run this marathon, just not this year. I nodded as people told me how great it was that I hadn't given up on my dream and that they really admired my persistence. Running successes and failures both invite clichés.

The manuals are coy when it comes to pulling out of a marathon. They're full of homilies about injuries—but not about slacking off. The disheartened novice is advised to keep her chin up, to keep striving. Not long after starting to run, I'd become attached to the fantasy that I might stay on an arc of steady improvement, that if I kept training more or less steadily, I would find myself to be infinitely perfectible, turn into a lump of speedy gristle, and scoff fondly at my novice years. I had let myself get giddy thinking about what I might be able to be or do if I could run a marathon. That's nonsense: but when I opted out, I was made uncomfortably aware of my self-improvement failures.

I'd been a running dilettante who'd placed too much emphasis on pleasure, treating my runs like sightseeing opportunities, not training challenges. A bigger problem was that I hadn't calculated my long runs according to distance, but according to time. On slow days I hadn't run far enough. I'd just been pleased that I could run for such a long time.

Some runners worry over wasted miles: runs that contribute nothing to a training routine except fatigue. Those are the runners who, I imagine, maintain a perfect balance between calories consumed and expended, who know exactly how far they've run each week. They only slack off when injured and make up their runs later. This is, admittedly, a sensible approach. I'd failed to string out my energy over the training period and so hadn't found the balance between not doing enough and overdoing it. Like a credit addict, I had wasted many, many runs by sticking to a too-slow pace and failing to track my distances. If I'd been subject to a performance review, this failure to monitor my key performance indicators would have been noted. *You can't manage what you don't measure, young lady. Don't forget the metrics.* That kind of talk makes my blood foam—and yet, it all added up. Or rather, it didn't.

A year later, I was ready to give it another go. I'd returned to regular running and finished a few more half marathons.

Lapping the park in the early morning still brought me great pleasure. I was ready to swallow my doubts and try again. I entered another marathon.

*

I was aware that my obstinacy about the kind of training I would and wouldn't do was hindering my progress. I loved long, floating runs, and I hated sprints and hill drills. To prepare for what I had hoped would be my first marathon, I'd avoided strength training altogether, though my running manuals were of one voice: do some strength work. Everyone I knew who'd run a marathon agreed with them.

As I contemplated this next marathon, I decided that I'd go back to the gym, twice a week, and build up my legs—whatever that meant. "Squats and lunges," Brendan from work had advised. "Get into them. You'll be fine." The quiet Kings Cross gym I'd first frequented had shut down by then, so when I found a leaflet in my mailbox offering an amazing deal at a corporate chain, I signed up. I told myself that I could even run on the treadmill for old time's sake if the rain set in; I'd have one fewer excuse for skipping a training run.

When I'd last joined a gym, I wasn't able to run 2 miles at a stretch, and the gym hadn't been as awful as I'd expected. Now, my body had changed; I had changed. I was reasonably fit—fit enough to run half marathons—so what did I have to fear from a gym? Plenty, it turned out. I thought that running in heavily branded half marathons had prepared me for intense manifestations of mass fitness culture. I was wrong.

In the locker room I was assailed by ads for tooth-whitening and skin-bronzing treatments, for cosmetic surgery and non-surgical facial enhancement, for protein shakes and delicious meal replacements. These exhortations to self-transformation horrified me. The place reeked of sanitized bodies working hard to turn themselves into better bodies. Fat was the enemy. I wanted to leave guerrilla copies of Susie Orbach's firecracker book *Fat Is a Feminist Issue* on the benches and flee. I botched the dress code too, wearing a baggy old gray T-shirt printed with an image of Clint Eastwood from his Sergio Leone days. My thousand-yard stare hit the mirrors and reflected back to me a schlubby mess, out of place in a crowd dressed in bright synthetic fabrics. The sonic environment was that of a manic dental hospital: metallic thuds and human grunts against the whine of high-energy remixes of terrible dance tracks. Was I reading J. G. Ballard at the time? That might have been why I experienced the place as some kind of psychosexual dystopia.

I picked a route through the cardio room and looked for the switch to flick this flesh-and-metal madness into something I could recognize. I've heard people say they prefer to exercise at the gym because it's a private space, but this all felt very public. The treadmills were shoved against enormous windows that looked out over Kings Cross. Across the road stood a pub with a rooftop bar. I'd sat up there drinking spritzers on many apricot-hued summer nights, watching people flog themselves on the machines under fluorescent lights. Were those tread-millers looking back at me, wondering how I could abuse myself like that? I didn't put myself in their place to find out. I chose the treadmill farthest from the windows and kept my head down.

Metrics pose no problems for gym-goers: everything is

geared for measurement and efficiency. At this gym, even the layout was designed for peak performance, with treadmills and step machines packing the cardio room to maximum capacity. The free towels were exactly the right size—which is to say, too small. The exuberant young man who took my details was convinced that I'd see returns on this wise investment in my body very soon. His promises about how good all this exercise would be for me, if I'd just lighten up a bit, were much more grandiose than any future benefits I might have hoped to gain from running a marathon. Forget the marathon—if I stuck to my gym plan, I'd be more productive at work, I'd be on the path to incredible hotness, whatever mating dreams I entertained would be realized. I could have it all! No need for me to cultivate good habits: here, it was inputs and outputs, drills and results. Friends tell me that this is exactly what they like about the gym: they turn up, work out, and go home feeling better. That's what I'd said to them about running in the park.

As a sign-up bonus, I was offered a few free sessions with a personal trainer. Let's call him Biff. He was younger and taller than me, and his tattoos were of the boorishly heterosexual variety. I'd broken the news that I planned to run a marathon later in the year without mentioning the fiasco from the year before. "You've got a lot of work to do," he said. "Running is a great way to lose weight, but I don't think the marathon's right for you. You've got the wrong body type. Sometimes we set our goals too high."

"Oh, I'm pretty determined," I replied, in what I hoped was an even, amused tone. *What would Violet Piercy or Bobbi Gibb have done in this situation?* I wondered. There were plenty of feminist icons in my mind urging me to tell Biff to fuck off. I asked why he was making me do bicep curls, and he laughed. "You're feisty, I like that," he said. "But you leave the decisions to me—I'm the trainer." He threw a medicine ball at my stomach and told me to show him what I was made of. I'm not sure whether it was supposed to be punishment for my intransigence, but I held that heavy ball above my head and lunge-marched lap after lap of the gym, driven far beyond my pain threshold by irritation. "Good work, darling," he said, and winked. The following day I couldn't sit down without clutching a table for support.

Session two involved an hour of crap advice that five minutes online would have debunked. "The tannin in tea sucks iron from your body. That's bad news for vegetarians like you. If you're serious about the marathon, the tea has got to go. Hope you like beans. I'll have you eating a lot of them. Farts! Farts! Farty farty farts! From now on, 4 liters of water a day—minimum. That trip you've got planned to France? If you don't get yourself into the mountains and run at altitude, you're crazy. I don't care if you're going to Paris to work, it's an altitude opportunity. Have you got a boyfriend? French men, watch out for them, eh? How about a fat test? If you're serious about the marathon, girls like you have got to think about body fat. Fat's a big problem—you need to be lean, but you've got to keep something in store."

I ran on a treadmill as Biff screamed at me and pushed the speed arrows higher and higher. "I want to see you sweat! Faster, yeah, faster. Stand up straight and don't slouch. Don't think I'm going to show you any mercy. Don't fight me, darling. Are you serious about this? Are you?" When I was done, he tried to hug me farewell. "Good girl."

An old negativity had surged in me, a child's bewildered fury at finding herself out of place. Running had transformed my ideas about my body—and here, that same body was construed as an enemy to be disciplined and controlled. Punishment as reward, self-loathing as motivation: I'd had enough. I declined to take up the third free session with Biff. Was I serious about running a marathon? Maybe, but it wasn't going to involve rebuilding my attitude at the gym.

I stormed home adamant that I'd never return and was thwarted even in that modest goal. In spite of my many requests that my membership be canceled, the gym continued to extract fees from my bank account. Finally, I climbed the stairs again and used my loudest, least impressed tone of voice to settle matters. It took years for them to stop calling and asking me if I was ready to return. In spite of our obvious personality incompatibility, Biff too pursued me with phone calls for months. Couldn't we give it another go? He was still prepared to take me on as a client. He'd give me a great rate. He was impressed by my attitude. I asked him to drop it and, eventually, he did.

*

When I quit the gym, I still hoped it might be possible for me to run a marathon later that year. I would just keep running and see how far I could go. I hopped on a plane to Paris, and took my sneakers and my marathon dreams with me.

Did I take Biff's advice and run at altitude on that trip? No, I did not. I was fed up with tests and ordeals. I'd done enough thinking about failure—if I happened to get to the starting line of the marathon, I'd deal with all the drama of potential failure then. I sat in a bar on the day I arrived and toasted my father, who had lived and died an unreconstructed Francophile, with a pastis. He'd given me a print of a Toulouse-Lautrec era advertisement for absinthe that had been tacked to his bedroom wall when he was a student. I'd stuck it above many desks and, as I worked, would look up to see a red-headed urchin stealing a glass of absinthe from the table of a glamorous courtesan, her bodice picked out in Campari red, as she entertained her admirers, only one of whom noticed the thief.

That particular Parisian afternoon fell in early spring, as the streets were beginning to warm up again. It was late night in Sydney, and my eyes were confused by the pale sunshine so I sat inside and stared into the past. What had I been doing in that gym? I shouldn't have been conned by that talk about self-management. If enduring a major catastrophe teaches you anything, it's that it's easier to maintain self-control and make good decisions when your environment is stable. Discipline may make sense in a controlled space like a gym—but it doesn't necessarily hold as a rule in a world where planes fall out of the sky, where the structure and figures of authority prove vulnerable to collapse. It can look like a crazy, desperate gesture.

I had no firm understanding of why my father had taken to endurance sports in his thirties, and if he had entered any events that he'd failed to compete in, I'd forgotten them. I suspected that if he'd entered a marathon, he would have finished it. Deliberations like these were not as painful as they once had been. I'd somehow endured the first horrid decade since Mum and Dad died, even if I hadn't run a marathon. I would never share a mid-afternoon apéritif with Dad in a cheap bar in Paris. He'd given me the taste for fierce, sweet aniseed, and it was in the hope of holding on to the vivid memory of him that I ordered another pastis. He would never answer my training questions, and we'd never get to have an awkward conversation about breaking points, about the unspeakable motivations of endurance athletes. If he'd trained for triathlons to cope with some deep hurt, he never told me about it. No matter how far I ran, that would remain unknown. And if my father kept me company that afternoon, my mother would some other time.

On that trip, I carried a sincere intention to run often. Running at home was easy, but I still found running in new environments difficult. I'd arranged to stay in Montparnasse and told myself that I'd run through the Luxembourg Gardens, just around the corner from where Gertrude Stein and Alice B. Toklas had lived and kept their salon. The problem was familiar by now: I couldn't face the dash through busy streets to get there. My habits were out of whack and I didn't know where to stash the huge ring of keys I needed to open the doors to my building and apartment. I had packed the wrong sunglasses. I didn't know where the water fountains were. The paths in the gardens were dusty, and if I tripped I'd graze my knees. And so I didn't run. Instead I walked for days, thinking about how all this walking was building my endurance.

I'd been utterly miserable when living in Paris half a decade earlier. Research for my doctorate had taken me there—along with the hope that my heart might be lighter somewhere else. The battle to turn that research into a thesis lasted several years; if a terror of failure had kept me going then, I hardly wanted to revive that brutal self-discipline to run a marathon.

Even though I hadn't smiled much when I lived in Paris, I think I would have snorted with laughter at the suggestion that one day I'd seriously be talking about running a marathon.

Now here I was, back in Paris, a runner who wasn't running. Instead of running, I was mulling over Gertrude Stein's incantations about continuity and repetition; instead of running, I was considering which of the Parisian artists and poets of the early twentieth century, women who had so captivated me, might have run marathons had they lived now. Stein, certainly not. Djuna Barnes and Jean Rhys, certainly not. H.D., possibly. Perhaps one of Natalie Barney's circle, perhaps Missy the music-hall star.

I bought a pair of shoes with heels that were too high, shoes that a runner should never wear, and walked up five flights of stairs in them to drink rosé with friends. "Who runs on the Left Bank?" I sighed as I dramatized my inability to run in the city of lights and lovers. We talked about wine and universities and unemployment and running and, by way of consolation, they told me even Parisians were going to the gym these days.

*

Later on that trip, in Lisbon, I came across a reference in a newspaper to Haruki Murakami's memoir about running and realized, with a jolt, that it had been more than a month since I'd been out running. Even with a few months to go before my second stab at the marathon, I had a presentiment that my training plan was over. I found out that Carlos Lopes, a Portuguese runner, had brought home the marathon gold medal from the 1984 Olympic Games, but that his win had been overshadowed by the first-ever women's Olympic marathon. None of this information urged me on.

Once more my plan was overwhelmed by place. Excuses not to run were easy to find in Lisbon. The square cobblestones were too slippery and often smeared with dog shit. The hills were too steep, the sidewalks too narrow. And anyway, I was utterly involved with reading David Foster Wallace's great book, *Infinite Jest*, an endurance undertaking in its own right. I lay on an uncomfortable cane couch with a scratchy polyester cover and read for hours each day, mesmerized. In his introduction to the edition I was reading, Dave Eggers wrote that it took him a month to read. I was pleased that I would finish it faster than him, mainly because I'd spent so long resenting Eggers. I had been given four copies of his memoir *A Heartbreaking Work of Staggering Genius* when it was published not long after the plane crash. These were kind gestures from people who thought that someone whose parents had both died suddenly might want to read a book by someone who'd had a similar experience. Eggers had turned being orphaned and loaded with new responsibilities into his own literary genre. Not only that, he'd also established a worthwhile publishing and education enterprise. All in all, he seemed to have done much better, under the circumstances, than I had. I'd read the book, unable to shake the sense that I should have made more out of my own disaster. Every time a silence was broken by a slightly tentative voice asking whether I'd heard of Dave Eggers, I'd snap that, yes, of course I had.

Now I read and let myself unravel through the improbabilities and kindness of *Infinite Jest*: tennis, addiction, diversion, yearning, recovery. In this other world, I forgot again about my idiotic race with Eggers. The running I love most involves this kind of forgetting—it's not an escape, but an immersion in a parallel reality. The book was a mirror and a maze, and to finish it so fast required an effort of crazed concentration that I found exhilarating. It recalled to me that fiction can be as transformative as physical exertion. By the time I'd finished it, I was less bothered by the weeks I'd spent not running, less hung up on having screwed up that first marathon, not so worried by the likelihood that my next effort might not work out. I might not know how to approach a marathon, but I did know how to make my way through a monumental book.

I resolved to hunt down a copy of Alan Sillitoe's short novel *The Loneliness of the Long Distance Runner* when I returned home. By distinction of being one of the only novels that's more or less devoted to running, it's probably also the most famous novel about running. I'd read it when teaching a course on post-war British literature and hadn't thought of it for years.

There's a 1962 film adaptation directed by Tony Richardson, starring a dreamy, angry Tom Courtenay. My parents would have been too young to have seen it in the theater, and I don't think they would have had any interest in looking up the acerbic '60s films of young British directors like Richardson. Their loss. What had stayed with me from the film were images of the protagonist, a loose-limbed young man named Smith, running alone in the British countryside, all stiles and hedges and benevolent trees. I remember how peaceful that running seemed, and how eloquent and expressive his movements were. (I wish that I could summon similar scenes from film history that feature young women running like this, safely abstracted.)

Sillitoe's book is often cited by running coaches as a touchy-feely motivational aid—a feat that requires some dextrous misreading. Why? Because in this narrative, the hero, who loves to run, throws a race. Smith is stuck in a borstal—a reform school for young delinquents (or a prison, depending on how soft your heart is)—and is granted permission to train in the countryside for a running competition against another institution. He's given this special privilege by the borstal's governor, who wants him to win the race as his proxy. The governor may have power over Smith, but he has no dominion over his inner life: "I'm a human being and I've got thoughts and secrets and bloody life inside me that he doesn't know is there, and he'll never know what's there because he's stupid." The physical pleasure of running is literally an escape from confinement and, as Smith's stream of consciousness narration reveals, it also enables a glorious mental flight: "as far as I was concerned this feeling was the only honesty and realness there was in the world."

On race day, Smith, the favorite, stalls just before the finish line. He's nobody's show pony, and his refusal to win is subversive and terrific. The opposite of the winners-are-grinners approach. I think of him when I bump into packs of runners jostling pedestrians out of the way, and when I walk past that slick gym, still full of shouting trainers. Who needs to win the race? What did I have to prove by running a marathon?

How could I explain to any running coach, let alone a knucklehead like Biff, that I'd let my training slide, walked a lot, read a long and wonderful book—and that I was now ready to start running again. That reading had make me think of running in new ways, and that running had taken me back to books I'd forgotten. In Sydney, I settled into a new running routine but I didn't manage to run a marathon that year. A month before race day, I demoted myself to the half marathon pack. No great crisis had arisen. Nothing was wrong with me. I wasn't injured. I wasn't terribly depressed. I simply hadn't done enough training. I ran a fast half marathon and, this time, it didn't feel so much like failure.

10

OVER THE LINE

I'd started out a hopeless runner with zero confidence and no expectation that I'd be able to run even 10 kilometers. I'd turned into an adequate half marathoner, a runner who knew how to train just enough to make the distance. I'd discovered that continuous, uninterrupted improvement was a pipe dream, that athletic alchemy was a myth. As much as I loved running, it hadn't reshaped me into a highly disciplined creature. I knew that I couldn't run forever. And yet, I still held on to this desire to run a marathon.

And then, one wet January Monday in 2011, on a slightly mopey whim, I put my name on a list to express my interest in running the New York City Marathon. A week later, I found that I'd been allocated a spot in one of the most famous marathons in the world. My entry had been approved so quickly that I didn't have time to think it over. This one, I was *not* going to fuck up. By reasoning that now appears a little shaky, I decided to run the Gold Coast Marathon in July that year by way of preparation. If I managed to finish that one—known for being an easy, flat course—then I'd start in New York in November without any pesky first-time nerves. In that year, I started two marathons—and finished them both. A triumphant narrative—finally.

By this time, I'd had lots of practice training for marathons. A weekly long run and two or three weekday runs. My long runs were longer, and I skipped fewer of the weekday runs. With the help of my smartphone, I tracked the distance of all my runs and was often disappointed to discover how short they were. In a notebook, I maintained a terse record: *Tues 12 km; Sat 17 (rainy)*. Not a clear victory for self-management, but a formidable advance, and a very useful one. I wish I'd kept more notes on the rich physical experience of running: how my feet felt when I took off my shoes, the sensation of rain on my face, the tightness in my shoulders. I stopped avoiding hills and added tiny sprints to my weekday runs. I practiced yoga as often as I could to stay flexible and strong. I didn't bother with the gym but, occasionally, when I was very motivated and in the mood for clowning, I lunge-walked a few laps of my apartment.

I'd never been to the Gold Coast, a haven for retirees and pleasure seekers just south of Brisbane. In my imagination, it was a bit like a gym, an anonymous backdrop where I'd be able to test out my marathon-running fantasy. As summer slipped into autumn, I ran around Sydney and tried to picture myself completing the first miles of a marathon not in Queensland, but across the Verrazano Bridge. If going to New York to run a marathon seemed ridiculous, then going to New York and failing to run a marathon would be unbearable. I was hitting snags with my visualization exercises—no one ran in the New York novels and movies that I loved. Still, the glamour of the big city helped keep me in motion. Each week I ran farther around the northwestern shores of the harbor, watching the leafy trees turn amber, then brown.

I ran until I was ready to line up and wait for the starter's siren on the Gold Coast in early July. The month before the marathon, I'd logged two runs over 18 miles, and I'd estimated the longest was about 22 miles. To run a slow marathon, that was about enough. I'd spent most of June at a film festival, loafing. My training tapered off, and I stuffed myself with pasta and potatoes each night. The fortnight before, I kept my legs limber with short runs and slept a lot. After all that rest and exercise, my body was made of elastic. I was all potential. If I wasn't going to run a marathon, I'd have climbed a mountain, or filibustered any crowd that would have me. If I'd started walking, I might never have stopped. The week before the race, I hopped around in a state of deranged invincibility, pulled tight with nerves.

I'd run my first half marathon with a brace of cousins and my aunt Anne on the sidelines. A happy collision of circumstances meant I was able to run my first marathon in the same company. On the eve of the race, we met in a hotel by a golf course that had been booked solid by marathon runners. The restaurant was full of leggy people eating pasta and buzzing with the lunatic energy that had been keeping me awake for weeks. Spaghetti with tomato sauce and a glass of rubbery shiraz for me. The waiter insisted that it was a meal for champions, and I laughed on cue. Ha ha, some champion.

In my room, I set the alarm for 4:30 a.m., took half a sleeping pill, and dropped off watching a rom-com about a stupid couple and their dog. In the morning, breakfast in an overlit hotel room: bananas, peanut butter, and honey on toast. I'd eaten this breakfast a hundred times before. A cup of coffee and a bottle of orange Gatorade. Off my head with sugar and nerves and caffeine.

It was dark when we arrived at the starting area. Anne hugged me and told me that she wished my father, her brother, was there to see all this, and I didn't flinch, because I would have been pretty pleased to see him there too. My cousin Danny and I watched and cheered as Anne and the rest of the troupe started the half marathon. Just then, I didn't care whether I finished the marathon; I was content to have finally made it to the starting line. Eventually, I waved goodbye to Danny too. A fast runner, he wanted to start near the front of the pack.

I waited alone as the sky lightened, bringing myself into focus as if through a lens, and saw a thirty-something woman wearing old red sneakers. She was rolling her feet inward and leaning on her inner arches, a nervous tic that kills the knees. Black shorts. Purple singlet. Green hat. I pulled back to include in the frame the tens of thousands of people gathered there on the starting line. The farther away it was, the more I looked like just another runner in a crowd of runners, and not like a freak who'd patched together a fallen-apart life and held on to the idea of a marathon as though it might pull her into a new reality. Who knows who else was waiting there? Former teenage cross-country champions out to give it another go; corporate types responding to a challenge from a colleague; marathon lifers, wizened by years in the sun; people shocked into running by divorce or illness; bucket-listers and goal-setters; a few who'd let themselves think this was the best way to shape up; dreamers; bewildered people with something to lose or to prove. Essayist Charles D'Ambrosio talks about "kindred doubts"—perhaps that's what brought us all together.

*

As I was warming to the new idea that I might have something in common with the runners around me, the emcee stuck to the script: *You're all bloody legends. Give yourselves a massive cheer! This is an ancient tradition, and you're running in the footsteps of heroes. Here we are, continuing this tradition on the beautiful Gold Coast.* On he went. The marathon is about as ancient as the typewriter or the motion picture camera; that is, entirely a product of modernity. Its reputation wouldn't exist without newspapers and photographs and news that whizzed across undersea telegraph cables. I doubted that those of us lined up to run on the Goldie shared much of the experience with the seventeen men who started the first Olympic marathon in 1896.

How different was it to run a big marathon in 2011? That race on the Gold Coast started early to avoid the heat of the day—and, I suppose, to minimize traffic disruptions. In Athens they didn't start till two in the afternoon. When they did, a revolver shot sent them on their way. *Yeehaa.* The competitors were given milk and two beers three hours before they started running—early marathons were convivial events with plenty of booze. Some runners were passed beakers of wine and cognac as they ran by assistants riding bicycles. These days, you see every flavor of energy drink being swilled before a marathon, but runners tend to hold off on the harder stuff until the finish line.

The first winner, Spyridon Louis, had prayed and fasted the day before the run, and had reportedly eaten a whole chicken that morning. Not many starters finished in 1896, whereas most of us on the Gold Coast did. A Frenchman, Albin Lermusiaux, and the Australian runner Teddy Flack both gave the Athens Marathon a good go—but each dropped out 6 miles from the finish line. Flack collapsed, punched a race official, and needed to be revived with a boozy eggnog.

Women weren't runners but trophies in 1896—or, at least, one of them was. Should a Greek man have won the marathon, a special prize was offered: the hand in marriage of philanthropist George Averoff's daughter. It's a lurid twist on Atalanta's story. Greece had been heavily in debt when it petitioned to host the 1896 Games and couldn't afford to build all the stadiums required. A public subscription didn't raise enough cash—and in stepped Averoff. A Greek man *did* win the race, but because he was already married, he and Averoff's daughter dodged a wedding.

Women stayed on the sidelines in all events at those Games, and the person we can thank for that is Pierre de Coubertin. He held strong ideas about women's participation in competitive sports in that he was strongly opposed to it; if there were Olympic officials who disagreed with him, they held no sway. Opponents to the participation of women pointed to their absence from the ancient Olympics. In this, they were at least partially right. Sources vary: one says that the priestesses of Demeter were given leave to participate in the religious festivities, another says that any woman caught watching the Games would be hurled off a rock at Olympus. As usual, when talk of the wondrous traditions of the ancients gets going, particularly in the early morning, it pays to be skeptical.

*

I bounced on the balls of my feet, so full of calories and fitness and anxious excitement that I thought I might shoot up into the sky and start to belt out show tunes. *Glimpses of stocking, something shocking.* I was Patti LuPone, and the world really had gone mad. I hauled myself back to the ground. When the gun fired, I inched toward the starting line, elbow to elbow with the crowd. A slow-mo long shot. By the time my foot carried the timing tag attached to my sneaker over the all-important sensor, I was giggling at the silliness of it all. I wanted to run, and run I did. For hours.

The first half of the course was a song and dance past the distance markers; the second was *Sturm und Drang* against a backdrop of ugly residential skyscrapers and flat dirty beaches. To begin with, I tried not to look at my watch to check my pace. I wanted to run slowly, oblivious to time, for as long as I could. This was my big race strategy.

About 6 miles in, at the end of a long, straight stretch, I encountered a lone woman atop a milk crate who was bellowing persistent encouragement to everyone who ran past. That she wasn't hoarse by the time I appeared astounded me. Entirely unself-conscious, she devoted her whole body to cheering. She could have been a roadside evangelist. *You're all amazing. Keep going.* I wondered why she was there, whom she was yelling for, and I waved at her as I ran past. *That's right, darling, keep going.* Her voice stayed on a loop in my head for a long time.

My mood changed. I became enraged, just after the 11-mile mark, when a man rode his bicycle onto the course and pedaled alongside a friend. The course was narrow, and I couldn't summon the speed to pass him. He lit a cigarette and smoked it as he rode one-handed, regaling his marathon buddy with last night's antics. I wanted someone else to upbraid him, to yell, *You imbecile, get off the course!* Over several miles, I composed a series of rebukes, not one of which I delivered. I should have lectured him on the history of women's running and his place in the long line of smug pricks who have impeded the progress of women runners. Where were the race officials? I couldn't face the prospect of initiating conflict on the course. He might turn around and hit back with some schoolyard fusillade. *It's a free country, mind your own business, you look like you're not going to make it anyway, what sort of puritan are you?* I needed my energy for running. I allowed myself only one tiny, passive-aggressive cough. Finally he rode off onto a side street.

I crossed the half marathon mark in good time—if, perhaps, a little too fast. And then, in unknown terrain, I panicked. I'd run farther than 13 miles many times, but never in a road race. How was I going to run another half marathon on top of this one? My glee completely evaporated, and I sank into a new mental environment: a grim swamp. Maybe I was cut from the same cloth as the smoker on the bike, not these real runners. I wanted to stop, to click my ruby-red sneakers against each other and find myself back at home, comfortable: halfway through a Victorian triple-decker, chortling at Trollope's public servants; halfway through a bottle of rosé, no matter that it was a winter's afternoon; halfway through a joint, amiably disconnected; halfway through a nap, a wheel of brie, a boring anecdote, a tureen of ratatouille, an argument with a neighbor—anywhere but partway through a marathon with 10 miles left to run.

I kept running. There didn't seem to be anything else to do. The finish line swung in and out of my awareness. As I got closer, it seemed to sway farther away from me. My memory of the last third of the run is weirdly estranged from my body, and I can't remember what my legs felt like, just that I was tired and unreasonably angry that I'd let myself imagine I might run this far. Somewhere around the 21-mile mark, even this got boring, and when I heard a Patsy Cline song that my mother loved over the PA, I swallowed my rage and started to laugh.

As I approached the finish line, more spectators gathered and drew themselves into the action. "Trina," which is what my family calls me, was marked on my bib, and onlookers started to cheer, *Go, Trina! Keep running, Trina!* I'd forgotten that this nickname was visible. As complete strangers quoted Forrest frigging Gump to help me along my way—*Run, Trina, run!*—I spluttered at the absurdity of it all, at this long, long road I'd run along. I was running a marathon and had less than 6 miles to go. I waved at the crowd and hooted to myself, astonished and delighted by the outrageous prospect that I, this I who had hated running for her entire life, who was so clumsy, who had been so sad, who had sunk so deep into the quicksand of grief, who had entered two marathons and hadn't managed to start them, this I was going to finish a marathon.

It got weird. Joyous, loving ghosts spurred me on. I was sure that I could hear the voices of friends on the other side of the planet cheering for me. I picked out faces in the crowd that I'd almost forgotten, and I was shocked to see them. *This isn't really her kind of event*, I mumbled to myself. *How strange that she's here. What is that guy doing on the Gold Coast? I thought he was in Chicago or maybe Santa Fe.*

A brilliant, mad state of mind took me through the final stretch. Loves lost and lives lost emerged from the Gold Coast underworld to watch me run. Each kilometer marker cordoned off one impossibly long stretch of road from the next. I spliced the kilometer in half—and the remaining 500 meters reached before me as a new expanse. I was an exhibit in a lesson on Zeno's paradox, and my body was time's arrow, always approaching, never reaching its destination. Clutching that arrow, I met again my dear friend Nigel, one of the ones who really was mad to live and mad to talk, who'd named a zine after Zeno; Nigel who, had he lived, would have stayed up all night talking about marathons and masochism and ecstatic bodies and fascism; Nigel, who died when a tumor swallowed his kind, radiant mind, and provided yet more callous proof that death undoes every paradox. I lost my breath thinking of all the laughter that would have churned through those conversations we'd missed.

What would I have told my mother about this sane, moving hallucination: *Mum, I'm squeezing through a tiny aperture trailing all my pasts behind me, and every day I'd ever lived I'm living again here on the Gold Coast?* She would have known that I wasn't born to run. She would have remembered me sobbing at all those dropped catches and desultory races. She would have known that for me, to start running was not to continue a tradition, but to break with the past, that a marathon signified novelty and hopefulness. I kept running. Would my grandmother have been horrified by the sweat crystallizing on my cheeks and told me to wash, immediately? *I can't stop now, I've got to keep running*, I protested. *I'll clean up when I get to the end.* I wanted more ghosts—they rarely visited me like this, and when they did, I shooed them away, scared. Running, I lost my fear. There was my father, cheering like a loon, just as he had when I'd played hockey as a kid and missed the ball with every swipe. I waved and kept running.

This was supposed to be a rehearsal. I ran the whole stupid course to the end, raising my hands in the air when I crossed the line as some idiot runner would do, as I never thought I would. My aunt and cousins whooped and thundered while I cleared the timing strip in a mess of tears, sweat, and relief. In the photos taken at the finish line, my face is red and I'm very out of kilter. My left hip hurt, so I was leaning hard to the right; it looks like an awful injury.

The raving state passed, and I found myself in delighted shock. Someone gave me a banana, which I ate, and then I made my way to the people, keys, and cards that connected me to the world. After running for four hours, even these basic tasks seemed gigantic, tremendously important. I sat down with my cousins, bamboozled by the sudden cessation of exertion. I was still, but far from calm. The chemical reactions provoked by running for half a working day send weird spasms through the body. My doctor cousins tried to explain this, but I was too wired to take it in. Around my neck, a volunteer had hung a medal. Forget faster, higher, stronger: everyone who runs a marathon gets a medal. I'd insisted I wasn't in it for the glory but I didn't take off that medal until we returned to the hotel and I sloughed away the grime of the morning in the shower.

11

A ONE-SENTENCE SUCCESS STORY

I didn't know what it all meant, but the desire for that marathon to mean *something* took on a terrific urgency, one that fortunately diminished as the stiffness melted from my legs. All the training guides make a circular promise: once you've finished a marathon, you will become a marathon runner. What could this possibly mean? What did crossing the finish line mean to me?

That afternoon, as I traipsed through the airport with Anne for our flights back to Sydney, I had no idea. Had I some great insight into how that big run fit into the big story of my life, I couldn't have put it into words. If I drew my awareness to any one part of my body, I found an ache there. Heat and color flushed over my cheeks and chest. I watched a pair of hands futz through the ticketing process as if they belonged to someone else. To step down even a single stair, I needed to clutch a railing. Feverish, I could almost have convinced myself that this glowing state of pain marked the final stage in my metamorphosis into a marathon runner, that I was about to shed my old skin and board the plane in a new body.

I tried not to think too closely about the commitment I'd made to a repeat performance of the show. The only reason I'd entered the Gold Coast run was to chase away my doubts about the NYC Marathon. If that was a warm-up, what kind of emotional explosion could I expect from the main event? Calmly, I rehearsed in my mind how it would go: I would run very gently for a month to recover; I would pick up my training as the winter lifted; I would run another marathon.

There are permanent ways to record having run a marathon, to claim the distance as part of your life story. Over the years I've seen plenty of marathon mementos etched onto the bodies running past me. Plug "marathon tattoo" into a search engine, and you'll soon be scrolling through galleries of photos of red, raw new tattoos, all with 26.2 at their heart, or 42.2 if the distance is measured in kilometers. Sometimes, the number is all there is to a marathon tattoo—discreet little digits on the ankle or maybe the hip. I've seen the magic number emblazoned on a medal or surrounded by a victor's wreath. I am taken by the ones with elaborate illustrations, by numbers fluttering on cherub's wings or being jogged along by jolly cartoon feet, burning up the skin with flames. I've seen the distance tattooed into a detailed commemorative ribbon, with the date of a marathon and the bearer's time squeezed in for completeness. I've seen 26.2 illustrated by funky retro images of running shoes, long hilly roads, and slogans like good old *veni vidi vici*. A subgenre of marathon tattoos involves Roman numerals, often with wonderfully incongruous decimal points: XXVI.II or XLII.II. The Romans have nothing to do with the marathon, but the anachronism speaks to the reputation of the event as being an all-purpose pan-historic Big Deal. Though I've never marked my body after a marathon, I can understand the impulse to do so. Marathons generate eloquent scars and sprains and limps—but a tattoo is a bold and deliberate declaration of how a body has lived. It is a one-sentence success story: *I finished a marathon.*

As I sat in the airport bar, watching the departure screens and nursing a glass of vino, I would've said yes to anything: a marriage proposal, a job on an oil rig, an ultramarathon, a full sleeve ink-job. My arms were so sore that the effort of lifting the glass to my lips seemed almost magnificent. For the next few days, that marathon zipped me between fatigue and mania; had I knocked back a few margaritas with some bad-living friends in the Cross, I might easily have woken up with the words *I ran a fucking marathon* tattooed across my clavicle.

*

Marathon—μάραθον—is also the Greek word for fennel. The fragrant feathery herb, growing wild, gave its name to the plain 25 miles from Athens where the Battle of Marathon was fought. And since 1896, the marathon has spread like a weed.

The Association of Road Running Statisticians (ARRS) started keeping records about marathons in 1910—fourteen years after the first was run, only 186 athletes logged a finish in one of the fifty-four marathons conducted worldwide that year. Marathons are now booming: in 2012, the ARRS counted 3,586 of them—and 1,608,848 runners who finished. An Australian man recently wrote a book about running a marathon in a different city every week of the year: his itinerary took him to Havana, Reykjavik, Mumbai, Belfast, Luxor, Chicago. Marathons have a slot in the global leisure industry that serves the desires of moneyed fit people. Enthusiasts can schedule their vacations around marathons: shopping trips to Paris and Tokyo can be combined with a marathon, as can East African safaris and trips to the North Pole and the Great Wall of China.

Marathons aren't the toughest endurance event an athlete can contest—they never have been. The brutal, days-long professional footraces of the late nineteenth century, corrupt as they were, were contested over much longer distances. The marathon hasn't been the longest amateur footrace for runners for the better part of a century either. The 55-mile Comrades Marathon—the one run by my cousins in South Africa—was established in 1921, twenty-five years after the first marathon. And no marathon is anywhere near as tough as ultramarathons such as the Badwater (135 hot miles in Death Valley, California), the Barkley (a crazed 100 miles in the Tennessee hills, with no aid stations and no track) or the Marathon des Sables (a six-day, 156-mile event run through the Saharan sands of southern Morocco).

There may be higher bars to clear to prove that you're invincible, but the marathon retains its rhetorical prestige as a marker of endurance. The easy adaptation of the word *marathon* to spheres that have nothing to do with running is evidence of its sentimental pull: if you want to emphasize that an activity is a slog, call it a marathon. A long week at work is a marathon in the office; pulling an all-nighter to meet a deadline is a marathon effort. Marathons are everywhere. Finish a marathon writing assignment and ask someone to buy you a drink. The suffix "-athon" has been broken off, like a branch snapped from a stem of fennel, and now works as a modifier that adds kudos to pretty much any time-consuming activity: shopathons, walkathons, talkathons, swimathons, readathons, dance marathons. Sit in a dark room and watch a screen for enough hours, and someone will call that a marathon too.

All this might suggest that a marathon—at least when the term applies to a running race—is an objective indication of a physical achievement, but the dimensions of the event were hardly established through rigorous scientific processes. The marathon that I ran on the Gold Coast was a little longer than the 1896 event—not until 1908 was the distance stretched to the standard 26.219 miles. Twenty-six and a bit miles is such a raggedy quantity that you might be forgiven for thinking it's an expression of the exact distance between two points. That's not the case. At the 1908 London Olympics, the race was started beneath the nursery windows at Windsor Castle—because the grandchildren of the king wished to watch the princess of Wales send the runners on their way. The starting line was moved back to accommodate the wishes of the royal family (hardly a win for the democratic tradition). The finish line stayed in its original position: in front of the royal box in the new London Stadium. This distance was standardized by the International Amateur Athletic Federation in 1921.

What's more, as I later discovered, runners have all sorts of systems for ranking marathons against each other. It turns out that not all marathons are the same. The Gold Coast Marathon is regarded as very easy because the course is flat and the weather tends to be mild. First-timers run it in hopes of a cruisy ride; experienced runners enter with plans to notch up a fast time. There are marathons with big hills, and those with notoriously slow climbs; marathons that are run in hideous heat, and those that hurl snow and ice at runners. In other words, no one runs the same marathon twice. And yet, the same question is asked of every single marathon: *How fast did you run it?*

*

I'm not a fast runner, and I do what I can to evade questions about speed. "Somewhere in the middle of the pack" is my standard answer. I told a friend that it took me over four hours to run the Gold Coast Marathon. "Four hours?" he replied. "My son finished in less than three and he's just a kid." Another friend let the time linger over the pints between us just long enough for the silence to seem a rebuke. "What's the world record these days—two hours?"

Speed is the easiest and most conventional way to measure a runner's performance—and a host of complementary techniques can be used to assess its worth. Good runners pay attention not just to their average speed over the course of a race or training session, but also to splits, their average pace per mile. I measure my runs in kilometers, and if I run 8 kilometers in under fifty minutes, I call them six-minute kilometer splits and claim an even speed of 10 clicks an hour. If I run those 8 kilometers in forty minutes, then I'm up to 12 kilometers an hour, my heart is pumping faster, the world spins around me like a crazy diorama.

As I've written, having some understanding of how far and fast I ran helped me prepare for my first marathon. Many smartphone apps are available to help gather running statistics—heart rate per minute, calories burned, meters climbed—and gadgets for gathering data about the body pro-liferate. If you're making progress, the counting can be hard to resist; even if you're not, it still feels like a game. I don't own a Fitbit, but I was startled recently to discover that my phone, bidden only by an operating system upgrade, had started to record the number of steps I take every day. No matter how I crunch the data, I don't seem to get much faster.

It may be thrilling to run at speed, but I don't do so very often. At the end of my first year as a runner, I finished a 10-kilometer race with a gentle, fast friend and logged what's still my fastest per-kilometer time in a race. It was a humid November morning, and florid storm clouds filled the sky. The gray heat made me dizzy; just before the finish line, I had to sit down for a few minutes. Even so, I was *fast*.

On rare occasions, propelled by some spiky cocktail of emotion and sugar, I've run with such furious determination that to halt has seemed like a greater effort than tearing into the space ahead. The blood throbs in my head, and I hear a child chant, *I will not stop, I cannot stop.* The world accelerates with me. After runs like this, I arrive home startled, shaky on my feet. I've flown so fast down hills into the wind that the momentum has turned my body into a glider ready to soar. Running on flat courses on still mornings, well rested and full of energy, I've experienced the lack of resistance to movement as something akin to ecstasy, and fought the urge to run even faster so as to conserve that energy and prolong that sensation.

I can see the beauty in speed and, now and then, the appearance of a fast runner stirs me to acceleration. On the right kind of day, if a really elegant runner with a body that moves like a liquid passes me, I try to match her pace for a couple of hundred meters, the longer to admire her gait. I pull my torso higher and hold my shoulders into firmer alignment in an aesthetic homage; I will more strength into my step and keep up for as long as I can.

This isn't how I ran the Gold Coast Marathon. I ran as slowly as I could manage at the beginning of the race to ensure that I'd be able to finish. Had I whizzed away on adrenaline and training and run a fantastic first 13 miles, I wouldn't have had a hope. With discipline and determination, I could up my averages, I suppose, but I'm never going to be really fast—and if I appraised my running experiences solely through the metric of speed, I'd be miserable.

Career athletes can be forgiven a focus on speed, but from everybody else the focus on competition and speed seems utterly ridiculous. At first, I found the quick questions about my pace a little gauche, and I still marvel if they're laced with competitiveness. When committed, gifted runners compare their performances to mine and smile smugly to find themselves the faster, I'm never sure whether to tell them that outrunning me is a paltry achievement. One day I'll stamp my foot and shriek, *Find someone else to chase around the playground!*

*

The problem of the slow marathon runner is a perennial topic for opinion writers seeking to dish up a bit of controversy. Slow runners, they claim, are killing the marathon. I've overheard a few barflies give this line a whirl in person, though usually they're trying to rationalize not running in an upcoming race. Better not to run at all than to bear the iniquity of a slow time—that sort of thing. Slow runners pull back the entire pack, they reckon. This foolish argument is demonstrably untrue: for all the slow runners on marathon courses around the globe, the world marathon record continues to drop; more and more amateur athletes clock times that would have smashed a world record a few decades ago. The front of the pack is faster than ever. Worse to the complainers is this threat: that the achievements of fleeter runners—who, at the extremes, train until they vomit, whose marathons cost them knee joints, marriages, kidney function—are downgraded by those who do what they can, who are just happy to finish the race.

To me, complaints about slow runners often sound like proxies for objections to women running. Getting worked up about speed tends to put women in second place, even those who run spectacularly fast. Some women run faster than some men, it's true, but broadly speaking men run faster than women at every level of competition. At publication, the world women's marathon record is held by British runner Paula Radcliffe, who ran 2:15:25 in the 2003 London Marathon. Radcliffe would have been bested by only a matter of seconds by Sergei Popov, the male Soviet runner who broke the world record in 1958 with a time of 2:15:17 at the Stockholm Olympics. Runners of this caliber take just over five minutes to run a mile; I wouldn't be able to run even 1 mile that fast—neither, I'd wager, would most readers of this book.

If my slow pace and low ambitions raise eyebrows, Radcliffe, who is breathtakingly fast, has been subject to extraordinary scrutiny. In 2011, the International Association of Athletics Federations (IAAF) changed their criteria for the women's world record, decreeing retrospectively that it could only be set in women-only events. Radcliffe's fastest time, set under "mixed conditions," was relegated to world's best, and her slower 2005 Chicago Marathon time became the record. The lingering insinuation is that her top speed wasn't quite her own doing, that she owed it to male pacemakers. The rules for the men's world record remained the same. Later that year, the IAAF reluctantly issued a special ruling to restore Radcliffe's 2003 time as the world record. A range of opinions have been put forward about whether mixed conditions give elite women an unfair edge, and although Radcliffe's record stands, future contenders must run in women-only races.

Another example of the convoluted dynamics of women, speed, and recognition: an Australian runner, Adrienne Beames, is sometimes recognized as the first woman to have run a sub–three-hour marathon in 1971. Her time was disputed, as Beames—like Violet Piercy before her—ran the distance in a time trial rather than a race, so her name isn't in the record books. "Women don't usually run marathons" was the opening gambit of *The Age*'s report on Beames's run. "I just wanted to do something different," Beames told the newspaper. (The story wasn't exactly big news: it ran on page 14, beneath a picture of Collingwood footballer Des Tuddenham relaxing in the bath.) As if to reinforce Beames's point that women could run very fast, later in 1971, U.S. athlete Beth Bonner broke three hours in the NYC Marathon—and her time was recognized. At the beginning of 1980, the women's marathon record had dropped by thirty minutes (the IAAF credits Norwegian runner Grete Waitz with a time of 2:27:32 in the 1979 NYC Marathon), a staggering rate of increase in speed—but women still weren't allowed to race the Olympic marathon.

With the exception of She Runs the Night, all the races I've run have been conducted under mixed conditions. When the results are reported online the following day, each competitor is classified according to age and gender. I can find out where I finished relative to the whole pack and to women of my age—however, separate awards are given to women and to men.

Gender segregation by religious organizations is cause for sporadic outcry; in sports, it's a given. Reporting of gender statistics in the workforce, for example, or in universities, serves a greater analytic purpose: gender can help us understand the dynamics of these institutions. In sports, the biological fact of smaller lungs and less muscle mass makes splitting men's competition from women's a no-brainer. Doesn't it? Men run faster; they hit tennis balls harder; the bodies they slam against each other on the field are larger. Some notion of procedural fairness governs this thinking. Women competing against each other are on some kind of level playing field and therefore have a chance of proper recognition that wouldn't be available if they were competing against men. And yet, the fairness of the separation is belied by the outcomes: wherever we look in sports—marathon running, tennis, soccer, cricket—we find a multitiered inequality that diminishes and marginalizes the achievements of women athletes.

The "natural" appeal of speed and strength complements nicely the cultural hold of patriarchy. Men's sports are better funded; male athletes are paid more than women; they compete for bigger prizes and sponsorship deals; media outlets devote the bulk of their sports coverage to men. Women athletes—just a peg lower on the *citius, altius, fortius* scale—are disproportionately underrecognized.

To pluck just one scandal from a deep pit of grotesque examples: the Australian women's soccer team, the Matildas, went on strike in 2015 in protest against being paid far less than the minimum wage for their full-time training and game schedule. Their vice-captain was receiving welfare payments; she reflected to a journalist, "I'd just be cleaning toilets going, 'Oh, if only I was a boy I'd be able to not have to do this and live comfortably.'" Finally, a deal was negotiated that gave the players a living wage—but only a fraction of the income enjoyed by their male counterparts, the Socceroos. That the Matildas were vastly more competitive on international rankings than the Socceroos didn't seem to matter much to the sport's governing authority.

Such stories make headlines, but women athletes are soon displaced when football fever hits, or when the men's Wimbledon final is played. You could fill several shelves with books about the men's marathon and male distance runners; relatively few have been written about women distance runners and almost all that have are autobiographies. Most sports writers, both literary and journalistic, focus on men's sports at the expense of female athletes. The exceptions aren't enough to break the trend. I asked a group of peers on social media to point me in the direction of interesting essays about sports— not one recommendation was about women's sports.

The priority accorded the fastest and strongest shapes a history that has demanded women athletes prove their worth in a thousand insulting ways—and then ignored them. Why was it that race officials in the 1970s slowly started to change their minds about women marathon runners? What tipped their thinking? Not the fact that many women demonstrated that their bodies were quite able to cope with the training load. Not the fact that women ran marathons without collapsing, and before and after bearing children. No, this empirical evidence was insufficient.

Scientists needed to declare an official shift in the status quo on knowledge about women's bodies. No male athlete has had to endure such a convoluted greenlighting process. Concerned that marathons weren't well understood from a scientific or medical point of view, the New York Academy of Sciences devoted its 1976 conference to them. The immediate backdrop to that conference was the intensifying campaign for a women's Olympic marathon, alongside the passage of the Title IX equality legislation in the United States in 1972: laws that prohibited sex-based discrimination that had a particular impact on women's athletics. Delegates, most of them male, finally agreed that no persuasive scientific evidence existed that marathon running was bad for women. They voted unanimously on the following resolution:

> That it is the considered judgment of the participants of this conference that a women's marathon event as well as other long distance races for women be included in the Olympic program forthwith.

I think back to one of the captions on that famous photograph of a race official trying to drag Kathrine Switzer off the

Boston Marathon course: "Chivalry prevails." Male experts needed to open the door for women athletes, medal hopefuls and, ultimately, average runners like me.

The milestones were all lugged into place by men; intrepid women distance athletes were trailed by groups of officials carrying sheaves of arguments as to why their achievements shouldn't be recognized. And the shoddy treatment of female athletes continues. Sports officials are still bothered by fast women—and women's sports are still treated as secondary to men's. As if that weren't sufficient outrage, those of us at the other end of the speed spectrum are upbraided for running too slowly, shamed for not trying hard enough. I've met plenty of runners who are astonished by my lack of ambition, who can't understand why I don't want to get faster. I could point to the hassle that elite women runners endure, and ask why I should bother. Women who run long distances are defying cultural norms that restricted their mothers and grandmothers to more ladylike activities; now it seems that women like me (and yes, a lot of men too) must conform to a different expectation: to commit to personal improvement, to hunger for a win.

Did I want to run faster in New York than I had on the Gold Coast? I suppose so—but much more immediate was my desire to finish the race.

*

With a few charismatic or celebrity exceptions, sports history celebrates winners. Who remembers runners who didn't place? To make the official history books, what matters is how fast a runner reaches the finish line. In starting my own account of running a marathon decades before I loitered at its starting line, I've already broken the rules—but all my beginnings and false starts are as important to me as the races. Had I spent my teens playing netball and actually catching the passes that were thrown to me, I would have become a different runner. Had I spent my twenties arguing with my parents and not making sense of their absence, I might not have become a runner at all. To start the story of my marathon-running in my thirties would lop off too much.

When I was twenty, the age a lot of the women who've held marathon world records got started, I wasn't training for races—I was hissing about patriarchy and scribbling feminist slogans on toilet doors. I was angry about hierarchies based on strength and speed, angry about all the restrictions women are expected to swallow. All that rage, surely, cast me as a runner. I was fed up with my mother telling me to dress nicely and my father teasing me as I tried to articulate a political position. I was refusing to shave my legs and chucking the ideas of beauty peddled by cosmetics companies. To have worn a pair of sneakers sewn in a sweatshop would have been social death. Would that fragile, passionate, self-absorbed young woman recognize the person preparing to do something so indulgent as fly to New York to run a marathon?

I had rested for a few weeks after finishing the Gold Coast Marathon and, as planned, I resumed my training as the weather warmed up. I didn't have to prove myself with a qualifying time to enter the New York Marathon, although many do. There's no way I would have made the cut-off. I ran as a charity entrant and raised money for a human rights organization; I signed away medical liability on the entry form, of

course, but there were no questions to answer about my reproductive organs. The program featured profiles of a carefully
curated mix of prorunners, veteran marathoners, first-timers,
and athletes who'd battled the odds, as if to reassure doubters
like me that anyone can do it. The New York event had been
the site of some of the most vigorous campaigning about the
women's marathon, and I was proud to be running it. Each
week of training I ran a little farther, clutching for confidence
that I'd be able to complete the race. *Don't overdo it*, I'd been
warned—*just make sure you do enough.*

The week before the marathon, I flew into JFK and applied
myself to my first task: overcoming jet lag. Then, on my first
quick run around Central Park, it became apparent that New
York can be very chilly in November, especially in the early
morning. This shouldn't have been a shock, but it was.

I'd had to bow out of my last long training run in Sydney
thanks to unexpectedly intense heat. For reasons I can't remember, I set out in the afternoon rather than the morning,
and ran through the city parklands to the eastern beaches:
Bondi, Tamarama, Bronte. The glare from the ocean and the
bright evening sun left me dizzy and nauseated, and I needed
to lie down in a bus shelter for twenty minutes to cool off. I
had a $10 bill in my pocket, just enough cash to buy a bottle of
sparkling apple cider from a fancy deli in Woollahra. The staff
watched me with concern as I took a first draft, possibly because my uncouth, sweaty figure disrupted the clean lines of
their shop. I couldn't explain or apologize—the cider had set
off fireworks in my throat that made me cough.

The morning before I flew to New York, I swam in the swell
at Bronte. As I dried off in the sun, I scrunched my toes in the

sand, trying to picture these feet in a pair of sneakers, running 26 miles. The Pacific lay before me; I would have to cross first an ocean and then a continent before I started to run. What would I do in New York? I'd see old friends, visit the Frick, walk the High Line, meet a childhood friend of my mother's; I'd complain about the coffee, interview people at the Occupy protest, see movies in the morning, eat bagels, read Frank O'Hara. And, then, I would run a marathon.

My contemplations didn't steer me anywhere close to the practicalities of a massive seasonal shift, and I boarded the plane unprepared to run in freezing weather. I had packed a pair of uncomfortable leggings, but hadn't thought to pop in a warm hat or a shirt that would cover my arms. If it rained on me in New York, if the wind picked up, I'd be lost. I could buy new gear, but even I knew that it was a novice's error to run a race in untested gear.

I met a runner from Auckland in Manhattan who invited me to the opening of a shop in Greenwich Village selling New Zealand woolens. He was a finance guy; a friend of his from the consulate was organizing the event. A runner named Kathrine Switzer was going to speak. She was married to a Kiwi. Had I heard of her? Her husband was an English professor; maybe I knew of him? Yes, I'd read his book on the literature of running and wondered where all the women runners were. It wasn't the professor who interested me, of course—it was Switzer. I could hardly believe my luck. What did it feel like to run a marathon that bucked the world's expectations? I had my own tiny answer to that question but I wanted to hear hers.

Did Kathrine Switzer unlock the mysteries of the marathon for me and reveal my place in its history? She delivered a stump speech about her Boston run and her part in promoting the women's marathon; I think I'd read some key phrases in interviews elsewhere. I didn't really care. I was starstruck and, I have to confess, extremely amused at the incongruity of finding myself tongue-tied in a downtown sock shop, intimidated by an athlete.

The day before, I had been working as a journalist, interviewing Wall Street protesters for a story I never filed. And the last time I'd visited New York, I was a serious graduate student doing archival research for my doctorate. The people who daunted me then were academics, and my doubts turned on whether I'd ever manage to complete my dissertation. I smoked cigarettes under the stone lions that guard the New York Public Library and strolled around Prospect Park at the end of the day, giggling at squirrels. Now it was as a runner that I wriggled through the crowd and introduced myself to a very friendly Kathrine Switzer. I managed to squeak out something earnest about my admiration for her *as a feminist*. Switzer had just been inducted into the National Women's Hall of Fame; as she shook my hand, she told me that it was the greatest honor of her career. The Gold Coast had nothing on this.

That was Thursday night. On Sunday morning, I got up so early that the streetlights barely broke through the darkness. The bus from Midtown to Staten Island passed across empty city blocks hung with marathon banners and bright bunting. My normal routines had been left in Sydney. On the bus, I ate a bagel and a starchy banana, and scoffed an uncaffeinated espresso-flavored carb gel given to me by a man who really wanted an audience for a thorough account of his race plan. I told myself that I needed a very small cup of coffee to start the race; my only option was Dunkin' Donuts, and I watched the sun come up on that cold November morning, sipping filter coffee and eating a doughnut.

Marathons always involve a lot of waiting and the overture at this starting line was epic. If it took this long to start, how would I ever finish? I surrendered to the wait and let my mood billow. The air was still and the sky was cloudless: a perfect day for running. A soundtrack of New York classics played on a loop—Frank Sinatra, Jay Z, Billy Joel—and I sang along too. I'm usually impervious to the mass emotions that shear through crowds, but I couldn't separate myself from the sentiments erupting around me. A group of Dutch runners were singing songs and exchanging hugs as if they'd already run the race. Two women darted through the throng, high-fiving everyone they passed. I swapped life stories with a man from the West Village dressed in head-to-toe fluorescent lycra. This guy, I learned, had run oodles of marathons. He also ran a good line about this being the greatest marathon in the greatest city in the world—no offense, Sydney—and I was one lucky little Aussie to be running it.

All my runs around Sydney had brought me here, to another threshold. The fierce alienation I so often experience in big groups ebbed and left me standing in something like an ephemeral community. I never would have believed that blending into an international crowd of runners could produce such a wonderful sense of identity and potential. Why was I here and not holed up at home, watching *Double Indemnity* for the seventeenth time, missing my parents? How had I managed to start again?

The starting siren blasted from a bridge pylon, and my

questions disappeared. I forgot Sydney. I forgot the Gold Coast. I forgot all my missed starts and my big ideas about marathons and those stupid questions about how fast I could run. I just ran.

I ran with the city: up and down five bridges, past bands playing Puerto Rican hip-hop and Hasidic metal; past school brass ensembles and speakers hanging out of the windows; I ran from Staten Island through the long straight avenues of south Brooklyn and the remnants of last night's Williamsburg parties. I got a little broody and anxious in Queens, until the climb up and over the Queensboro Bridge into Manhattan brought me back into my body. I ran to the Bronx and then back over the Willis Avenue Bridge into Manhattan.

Two million spectators watch the NYC marathon, and I was part of the show. Surely not everyone cheering on the sidewalks was there to watch a friend. The cheers were exuberant and I regretted that my name wasn't on my shirt this time. "Go, orange shirt!" someone yelled. I waved in the direction of the voice, hoping it was me the yeller meant, and not one of the Dutch runners.

If this were a truly uplifting motivational tract, the run would have got better and better, and I wouldn't have stopped grinning for the whole 26 miles. It would have been effortless, I would have floated across the line, everything would finally have made sense. There were no hallucinations to carry me to the finish line, but the last few miles were painful. Not even the recent memory of meeting Kathrine Switzer—women's marathon legend *Kathrine Switzer*—could keep a smile on my face. By the time I was running the last 3 miles down Fifth Avenue, my hips ached. Cold sizzles shot up my calves, and no matter how I swung my arms, something hurt: the balls and sockets in my shoulders squeaked as if they'd run out of lubrication; my damp shirt had stiffened to a board and chafed the soft skin near my armpit; pain alarms sounded in my neck and upper back. My shoulders slumped with the weight of my hands, so heavy I couldn't lift them to swat a hank of sweaty hair from my brow.

Did I think about stopping? Of course. I thought of nothing else. I was long past reminding myself that I'd flown halfway around the world to run this race, that I couldn't possibly withdraw. My first marathon hadn't turned me into a running warrior, invulnerable to doubt and weakness. Comforts filled my mind, so mundane and childish it's embarrassing to remember them: the thick comforter on my hotel bed, pillows, sweet tea, warm water, potato chips. How to reach this softly furnished nirvana wasn't a problem I could solve. I couldn't have walked back to the hotel, even if I'd been able to hoist myself over the barricades. Dressed only in a singlet and shorts, now both wet and hard with sweat, I would have become very cold very quickly, and anyway, the sidewalks were clogged with spectators. I thought the matter through carefully. The easiest option was to keep running. Finishing that marathon wasn't a triumph of will over flesh—it was pragmatism. I kept running and, after an epoch, limped through Central Park to the finish line with nothing left in me but a desire to sit down.

The finish line of the NYC Marathon only marks the end of the running. It was as if I were a character in a work of experimental fiction: never starting, never finishing. An official gave me a medal, pretzels, water and a crinkly space blanket; she directed me to keep walking through what felt like both a maze and a prank. I could stop and have my photo taken if I chose, but I couldn't exit the maze. I couldn't see any way to climb out and escape. I walked several blocks north and finally was released from Central Park, only to turn around and pick a path south to my hotel.

It took me an hour to get there, and along the way I high-fived a new cohort of strangers and beamed at other runners like an afternoon drunk. I kept my space blanket wrapped around my shoulders and held on to my medal as if it were my lover's hand. I don't think I could have spelled my name; I couldn't walk in a straight line, and I held my arms and blanket out beside me like a pair of wings for balance when I stepped off the curb. Adrenaline spikes made me stumble in and out of the scant November sun.

I ordered a giant cheese and pickle sandwich at the deli next to my hotel. The guy behind the counter wanted to give me free prosciutto, thought that I didn't have the cash, that I needed more protein, that I deserved it because I'd just run the New York City fucking Marathon. It took a while for me to persuade him that I was good to pay for the sandwich, thanks. *Hold the meat. I'm a vegetarian. I've just run a marathon. I can't argue the toss. I need to eat right now.*

I walked into the hotel lobby with a carton of that sweet pink grapefruit juice that I've only ever drunk in the States and a sandwich so big I didn't think I'd be able to bite it. I ran a warm bath and took two bites of my sandwich. The phone rang—home—and I answered it, a salty, weary wreck. If this was what it meant for a slow marathon runner, an unambitious athlete to be part of the history of the marathon, I could live with it.

12

HITTING THE WALL

Running gurus sometimes advise first-time marathoners to visualize themselves moving easily over the finish line, and to return to those images when the going gets tough. The trick, apparently, is to picture yourself floating to the end of the race. It's a tactic to help cope with sorely delayed gratification: imagine the hard part is over; imagine your body is unable to resist the impulse to move.

I don't have the knack of conjuring these states of effortlessness. My visualizations of fluent movement are all interrupted by images of me tripping over my shoelaces, of dogs running into my path, of my extended family appearing out of nowhere in some fond, disruptive show of support. The state in which I finished my first two marathons was nothing like floating—I was a stumbler. By the time I reached the finish line, my limbs had long lost any grace, and joint pain had forced a readjustment of my body's axis. I looked desperate, effortful, and a bit mad. Although "flowing" and "gliding" are keywords for visualization exercises, the finish line is more often understood to be a dramatic site, one where we're tested, where we approach our limits. In other words, it should look like it hurts—and, usually, it does.

The most memorable finish line images are the ones that show a runner on the brink of exhaustion, as if she's almost given up but somehow managed to access a precious last drop of energy. Runners who cross the line limping, with nipples bleeding and tears streaming down their cheeks, are invariably greeted with huge applause. Agonized finishes have fascinated runners and spectators alike since marathons were first dreamed up. Remember Pheidippides, the model for the modern marathon runner? He ran himself to death.

A few blotchy images exist from the 1896 Olympics, but there is nothing from the finish line of the marathon. Journalists reported that Spyridon Louis collapsed in distress not long after he won the gold. He never raced again. While there's pathos in the story, photographs can bring a runner's pain to life for those who aren't at the sidelines. During the Olympic marathon of 1908, images were collected at the finish line that express perfectly the charisma and drama of the painful finish.

Like Pheidippides and Louis before him, the Italian runner Dorando Pietri almost killed himself finishing that marathon—right in front of the assembled international media. The press corps were conveniently situated to capture image after image of Pietri as he slowly collapsed, his face contorted in pain and his limbs seizing up. His last lap of the stadium took an operatic ten minutes. Pietri had been given a dose of strychnine by his trainers just before he entered the stadium: a common, if risky, practice at the time that effectively switched off the brain's pain receptors. According to a contemporary newspaper, Pietri "staggered along the cinder path like a man in a dream, his gait being neither a walk nor a run, but simply a flounder, with arms shaking and legs tottering." He hit the deck a few hundred meters from the finish and was "helped"—dragged—across the line to first place by officials.

As the cinematographers cranked their cameras and recorded newsreel footage, and the photographers leaned into their tripods to take front-page pictures, they made an important contribution to the visual lexicon of endurance: this is what it looks like to finish a marathon; this is what it's like to push yourself to the edge. The footage is easy to dig up online, and it's unpleasant to watch. How, these shuddering newsreels invite us to wonder, would we fare if we were in that much pain? Thirty seconds after the wavering Pietri was pulled over the line, an American runner, Johnny Hayes, made it under his own steam. Pietri was carried away on a stretcher—disqualified. He woke up in hospital a hero and received a special prize from Queen Alexandra for valor, even though Hayes took the gold.

The first marathon run in Australia had a similarly emotional ending. The race started at the Sydney Cricket Ground on April 12, 1909, while the Easter Show was in full swing. Thirty-one runners headed for Blakehurst Post Office and returned to a stadium full of spectators. They weren't disappointed: while the winner, Andrew Sime, made it across the line still looking fresh and vigorous, the man who followed him staggered to the tape, fainted, and was carried away on a stretcher. The *Sydney Morning Herald*'s report the day after the race pays due homage to the lineage of marathon hardies—and gives more space to the man who placed second and provided the crowd with a bit of drama than it does to the winner.

Finishes like these cap off narratives about marathons as a transformative process. Many coaches advise that marathoners should approach the finish line with nothing left in the tank. (I've no idea how they reconcile this with that "floating" visualization.) I've never pushed myself this hard, never run to the point of vomiting or losing control of my bowels, misfortunes suffered by many distance runners. When people say they ran a marathon to see whether they were up to it, I think they mean they're curious about this place at the limits of human endurance, the one captured in the pictures of Pietri.

By people, of course, I mean me. When I started running, I was curious about how I'd perform under this kind of pressure. Bailing out of two marathons shifted my attention to the starting line. Perhaps if I'd made it to my first marathon start without any bumps, intrigue about a big, bloody finish might have kept me going. This kind of thinking posits marathons and other tests of physical endurance as trial scenarios for adversity that most safe and sheltered runners are never likely to experience. Endurance through prolonged, painful exertion is a sign that we've tried hard to outrun whatever we believe is tailing us: sadness, a knight on horseback, a fear of failure. To endure is to abide, to outlast pain. Are we brave and strong and tenacious at our limits—or do we slow down, collapse?

*

Only once have I experienced a test of self, or some approximation of it, while running a marathon. I can't say for sure whether I passed or failed. During the months that I was reading about Pheidippides—the exhausted, run-till-you-die-and-die-ecstatic Athenian messenger—I was thinking about Browning's ideas of heroism: the crazy self-annihilation that runners are supposed to be able to achieve, the feats of pain suppression. This was a couple of years after my Gold Coast debut. I'd entered the Canberra Marathon, which takes place in autumn as the trees around Lake Burley Griffin blaze red and yellow. I'd had a great run in the Sydney Marathon the previous spring and had spent the summer running on national park trails, rather than on the roads.

Canberra should have been a good marathon for me: I'd run the course before and I knew it was reasonably flat. A clear day—but I turned up woefully undertrained. So much for a narrative of progress, of learning to prepare for runs and knowing your limits. Usual story: life was busy, and I hadn't set aside enough time for regular runs. Standard running advice is that you can muddle your way through a half if you've done it before, but not a full marathon. I was extremely irritated on the morning of the race, because I'd forgotten to charge the MP3 player that I hoped would distract me as I ran. I was nervous, and snappy too, because I knew I was poorly prepared. I avoided all visualization exercises.

Fifteen miles in, my knee began to twang with pain, and I decided to walk for a spell. I hadn't tripped or twisted anything—my joints just weren't accustomed to the distance. I'd completed a couple of slow 18-mile runs to prepare for this marathon, but I'd started the race too fast, wanting just to get it over with. Here, perhaps, is the first rebuke to the idea of a defining, single encounter with pain. This sudden halt was the consequence of many decisions taken in the months before the marathon—to stay in bed, to cut short my training, to post-pone a run—made worse by the foolishness of outpacing my training in the first 12 miles. And now I was walking.

I thought about Pheidippides as I hobbled, about the way he's been used as a teaching aid in lessons on endurance. And I thought about the valiant Dorando Pietri, knocked out by strychnine, battling on. I know that running marathons at all seems deranged to many people; as much as I enjoy running into a state of mindless exhaustion, those models of athletic self-sacrifice seem idiotic to me. I could jog for about a minute before pain caused tears to well in my eyes. As I adjusted my gait to take the weight off my knee, mismatched twinges rico-cheted around my thighs. Eventually, whatever mechanism makes the femur comfortably swing in the hip joint stopped working. Was this the kind of pain that sleek runners take ibuprofen to prevent? It would be both an exaggeration and a typical runner's cliché to claim that every step was agony; it wasn't, but my knee hurt, it *really* hurt, and I didn't want to run anymore. What sort of resilience would I have needed to keep running—and how stupid would I have been to court real injury? Surely stupider than starting a marathon without sufficient training.

I grunted along in this way for several kilometers and even-tually stopped at a rest station in a park. Something like this would probably have happened, I thought, if I'd elected to tackle those first two marathons instead of taking the sensible option and running the half; if I'd done that in Canberra, I'd already be finished, eating pancakes and drinking coffee in the sun. An older gentleman was in charge of the rest station—just a table with water in paper cups—and when I told him, not puffing but still a bit wobbly, swallowing my bad temper, that my knee hurt, that I didn't think I could run any farther, he gestured to a chair and handed me some water. "Do you need an ambulance?" he asked. I didn't. "Well, you're welcome to sit here for a few hours, and then we'll drive you to the finish line." I was faced with two equally dismal options: going on or staying still. I wasn't carrying a phone and was far too vexed to make a distress call for a lift.

Wait for hours or walk for hours? The people I know who've pulled out of marathons weren't faced with such a banal dilemma. They had good reasons for stopping: digestive explosions, snapped ankles, immobilizing pain. I started to walk again, not through any heroism of spirit but to bring this sorry business to a quicker close. I ran for short spurts and walked for long stretches. Slowly the pain in my knee retreated, and I could jog at a constant, glacial pace.

I met a South African man in his fifties who was also fighting the urge to walk. He was running his first marathon and, though he looked pretty fit, he told me he'd never run more than 13 miles at a stretch. I'd trained more than he had, at least. I jogged past a heavy-set man in his twenties with tattoos on his calves who lumbered forward slowly and seemed oddly happy to shake his head every few steps and say, "Fa-a-a-ark." When we were side by side, he turned to me with a beatific smile and said, "I'm fucking dying here, love. You have a great day." Were we competing against each other? Hardly—we were just sharing the road for a while. A stranger riding a bike along the sidelines offered me water and red Gatorade, and encouraged me to persist. I was startled by her kindness. I thanked her with the little warmth I had, but I still regret not being more effusive. It wasn't some powerful reflex of will that pulled me out of my cantankerous mood and back into the race, but these small, companionable exchanges.

I'd heard a lot about "the wall" when I started talking to other marathoners. It's beyond the point where you want to give up, and maybe closer to a state of exhaustion and depletion where rational decisions—to walk or to drop out, for example—aren't possible. If you hit the wall, you'll know you've hit it, they say.

The wall is the boundary of a bearable and familiar reality; beyond it, who knows? There, we might find out whether we can go on when everything that's held us together shatters. The news, perhaps, that a plane has gone missing, and that plane contained your parents. Other shocks: your child has cancer, your spouse is leaving, your position is redundant. Will we survive this shock? Will we make it over the finish line?

When I walked most of the last quarter in that dismal Canberra Marathon, disappointed and tired, I was greeted with cheers on the final straight. "You're doing great!" someone shouted. I was too exhausted to reply that I wasn't, that I hadn't trained enough, that I hadn't passed any psychic test, that I'd had enough. It wasn't the wall I hit on that run—just the direct consequence of undertraining. I'd conjured an encounter with the wall as an heroic test of determination, an opportunity to show that while I might not be sporty, I sure as hell was gritty. My conviction was that I had the necessary reserves of whatever I'd need to see me through a few hours of arduousness; giving in to a minor injury on a long loop around Lake Burley Griffin wasn't what I had in mind.

I didn't need to botch a marathon to know what it's like to endure pain that seems endless and unbearable. I didn't need to hit a wall either. I wonder now if I looked a bit like Dorando Pietri in the years after my parents died: staggering toward thresholds that seemed arbitrary—birthdays, graduations, new jobs; bombed to the edge of consciousness. Would someone else have sat down on the track and refused to go any further? *How did you keep going?* people asked me at the time—and, later, *How did you not give in, collapse?* A curiosity about the frontier lands of pain lies behind questions about both grief and marathons. Many people think of grief as something like an encounter with the marathon runner's wall: a defining and lonely test of self that, once mastered, yields immediate recovery.

I'm still suspicious about the wall, but I know that grief is nothing like that. I felt alone, but I wasn't; small flashes of kindness have brightened even the solitary business of marathon running. There was no single moment of unbearable difficulty that I survived, only to turn back with relief and understand that a wound had closed. I've found it enormously satisfying to finish races—but every finish line, whether it's been a skirmish or a cinch, has just marked another beginning, another shift in the parameters of the possible. If there's any analogy to be drawn between marathon running and enduring grief, it shouldn't turn on one great exhausted clash of will against circumstance. It should accommodate a million training runs, aches and doubts, stops and starts, setbacks, tiny advances, odd connections, and, ultimately, not triumph, but joy and renewal.

*

It's as obvious to the absolute beginner as to the veteran marathoner that running engages the mind in vivid and surprising ways. Trying to express the holistic experience of running requires something like a trapeze to swing from one proposition to another—it's just the body at work, legs, lungs, core; no, it's the mind that keeps the body moving. But perhaps the mind itself is more muscle than mystery. And if running is an experience first of the mind, what happens to the body? From what spring flows the discipline needed to withstand pain? Questions like these drift through my consciousness when I run; my body brings them back to me when I'm weary and thinking about stopping. What would it take for me to run harder—a stronger mind or a stronger body? If my lack of running ambition is a failure, is that failure located in my guts or my brain or my past? And if that lack of ambition doesn't torment me, perhaps the failure collapses like a spent athlete, leaving me to pick out my own path. Such fragmentary thoughts on corporeality have brought me into a much happier physical existence; I don't see my clumsiness as a betrayal by my limbs anymore; I understand fatigue not as weakness but as feedback; I hold no desire to escape embodiment.

For feminists, questions about the mind and body aren't just pathways to running faster—they're also a way to understand the hierarchies that have structured gender. Controlling bodies is exactly what patriarchy does to women and queer people. Incitements to run harder and push through pain are in harmony with the constant exhortations to women: *Regulate your weight and appearance! Ignore hunger, ignore suffering, ignore anger!*

What do we lose when we cut off our sensitivity to pain? In Western traditions, carnal, corrupt women's bodies have been disciplined by the clarifying minds of strong men. *Mind over matter!* The prescriptions are exhausting, oppressive: running ever faster, impossible graphs of self-improvement, performance willed from unwilling limbs, mastery of pain barriers, the conquest of vulnerability. Who needs it? For some, wrestling discomfort keeps them in motion. Not me. What I love is running, just running. It's true that I was suckered by marathon magic for a while, that I ran in thrall to some notion that twisted bowels and screaming joints might represent a peak human experience. That view now seems incredibly myopic. There are better ways to map the pleasures that running has brought me; I've come round to a gentler approach.

Actually, the things I love about running are what many other writers love about walking: mental spaces cracked wide open by movement, new relationships to space, the body transformed into a medium of perception. It may be that the literature of walking resonates with my experience of running because I'm not a fast runner. For the walkers who traipse through the history of literature and philosophy, a slow pace can be revolutionary: ambling undermines the imperative to work, to produce, to earn. Similarly, running slowly is a powerful way to disobey the injunctions to discipline the body, to whip pain and fatigue to a pulp. Walkers find new ways to see the world and understand their place in it; that's how I think about running—and obviously it's easier to run steadily than like a woman under attack, and much more relaxing. There's less cause to suppress protest from the joints and the lungs. Blood sugar doesn't plummet in such a precarious way. It's safer, as the runner is less likely to slip, overdo things, or overstrain. If I threw my all into performance, if I sought out brutal, painful scenes at the finish line, I might miss out on the new worlds materializing around me as I run.

The first spaces that opened to me as a runner were urban. I found new lines of sight on gorgeous, greedy Sydney. I invented myself as a roving geographer and ran along the same paths each week, with set detours to see plants in bloom and mosses tumbling down stone walls. The boundaries of one run bled into the next as I fixed points on my new map of the city, visiting them again and again. I became attentive to the shifts in mood from suburb to suburb, the distinctive shapes of sidewalks and fences; a witness to the battle between the built environment and the skies, the sea and the trees. I ran on roads and sidewalks, and found myself an animal presence in the city, unburdened from the rate-paying, form-filling, and voting that comprised my responsibilities as a citizen. I was often tired and my legs often ached, but I was never bored.

Later, I moved from the inner city to a tiny village hidden in Sydney's southern rain-forest fringe. Here, I began to run on fire trails and slippery tracks built for hikers. The Coastal Track in the Royal National Park became my regular running path; it dances along the coastline for 18 miles from Bundeena to Otford, through heath, rain forest, low scrub, tall eucalypts and beach.

Off the concrete and asphalt, running has allowed me to enter into a demanding dialogue with my surroundings. Plenty of runners who started off on the road abandon the racing circuit altogether in favor of trail running, and I can understand why. The exchange between a runner and her environment is greatly intensified off-road. Each step requires concentration. Running down a muddy hill, my thought narrows to the placement of my foot. Where will it fall? Will the ground hold? Will I slip?

On the Coastal Track, the headlands are steep and treacherous, and loose rocks spray from the paths. A metal grille path has been raised over the slick mud alleys through scratchy heath, but clumps of sword grass still slice at my calves. I wear heavier shoes to absorb the impact of rocks and branches underfoot, and to protect my soles from sharp stones. I carry water with me in a pack. Headphones and sunglasses just get in the way—so my apprehension of the world is unfiltered.

Even after weeks of fine weather there's plenty of mud, and on most of my summer runs I worry about snakes, mistaking sticks for scaly bodies and birds rustling in the undergrowth for slithering. One summer, the cicadas were so loud I could barely hear the padding of my feet. I sometimes fret about being alone in the bush and pursued by anonymous assailants; if warnings circulate about women running without a chaperone in city parks, there are even more alerts about lonely national parks. But mostly, I worry about falling over. There's poor mobile phone reception along the track, so if I fell and twisted my ankle or tore the skin from my calves, I'd have to figure out my own escape route.

I return home covered in mud, my body salt-sticky with

dried sweat rills. Leaves and twigs tangle knots into my hair, and the stray branches that lash my calves and exposed arms leave scratches and sometimes bruises. If it's been particularly wet, I pull leeches from my ankles—a bloody finish to a run. The next morning, I wake up with the peculiar muscle strains from running up and down very steep hills and, often, aching feet.

If the running changes me, my body also leaves marks on the tracks. I slip on the path and deepen the puddles. I pull down branches to help me stay balanced, and strew rocks and leaf litter with my feet. When I kick a branch heavy with blossoms, I tell myself I'm helping to spread the pollen. I am slowly learning the names of the plants, and one day I hope the flora will be as familiar to me as the cottage garden plants that my mother loved so much. I look out for tiny native orchids, dainty as violets, and for flannel flowers. As winter hatches spring, bells hang from the heath, and the enormous Triffid heads of Gymea lilies open red above me. On my breaks, I cut through the trees to the spaces at the edge of the escarpment, and stretch my arms out to the ocean—a hundred meters below—like a figurehead, my ship the forest behind me.

The wildlife I terrify. Parrots shear through open paths ahead of me. Dotty little fairy-wrens scatter at my approach. I've seen a few snakes and many more species of lizards: skinks, water dragons, and geckoes, all trying to put some distance between themselves and my clomping feet. On weekday evenings when the track is clear of bushwalkers, I sometimes catch a glimpse of an echidna truffling in the dirt. Swamp wallabies live near the beaches and, at twilight, curious possums emerge. My presence is that of a great clumsy predator. Catbirds and lorikeets and magpies wheel above me as I trample on ants' nests and grind moss from the rocks. It's a shock, on returning to concrete paths, to discover that the surface offers so little resistance.

*

Before I even set foot on a treadmill, I wanted to know what it would feel like to keep running through the many permutations of mood and desire. This regular practice of endurance has been vastly more rewarding to me than chalking up personal bests. And so I'm ambivalent about framing my one conventional marathon success story—my fastest marathon, the one in which training and racing were most closely aligned— as my personal best. Perhaps it should have been the centerpiece to this book, but it feels more appropriate as a coda.

This was the marathon I completed before screwing up in Canberra, on home turf on a dazzling spring day. I'd twice entered the Sydney Marathon, and twice failed to start it. This was the marathon I'd watched my friends finish all those years ago, marveling at their resilience. That they had sailed over the finish line after running 26 miles seemed nothing short of extraordinary. They were made of different stuff than I was, I thought; they might have featured in parables about strength and persistence, whereas I was a weary, emotional mess.

The intensity of their endeavor stayed with me. I'd started the half marathon that's run on the same day as the Sydney Marathon many times. Shivering in the morning shadow of the Harbour Bridge, I'd watched the marathoners preparing— jealous not of how fast they could run, but how far. For me to be lined up in the muster area of that marathon, waiting for the starter's horn, was an index of many advances. As I waited, I swallowed a few last mouthfuls of sports drink, and rolled my head back and around to loosen my shoulders. I checked my shoelaces and stretched my hamstrings. I was relaxed. By now, I knew how to run a marathon.

The Sydney Marathon traces the lengths of roads very familiar to me: I was home. I reckoned that over the years I'd been running, I had covered the first stretch of the race—across the Bridge and into the city—at least a hundred times. I knew the view through the Heads to the Pacific, and I knew the points and bays that led to Parramatta on the west. I'd run along those paths on cold mornings with only a few dog walkers and cyclists for company. On this day, though, the streets were full of runners and noise: the music amplified to pump-up levels, the percussion of feet hitting the pavement in thousands of distinct rhythms, and the gasps, coughs, and snorts that are the ambient soundscape of a marathon.

I looked out for my sisters and my cousins, but saw only strangers on the sidelines. I ran with intermittent pain and doubt and the value of that pain and doubt evolved as I ran. And still, my confidence boomed because I had a story to tell about every street that rolled beneath my feet. When I became weary near the Inner West, I let the memory of the houses I'd once inhabited distract me. I'd *lived* here: slept, washed, wept here. What an intimate connection my body had to these streets. I ran past buildings that had once been filled with parties, and boarded-up pubs that I'd sloshed around for years.

If only I could take that lost young woman by the hand and convince her to run with me. I laughed at the idea of this marathoner walking into a warehouse gig and preaching the gospel of endless steady movement to a bunch of drug-fucked club kids—and then I sobbed because that past is out of reach, and I could no more care for my younger self, that daughter without parents, that sad creature tense with denial and confusion, than I could pluck my mother and father out of the plane in which they were traveling when they died and restore them to their seats at opposite ends of the family dining table.

I kept running, across the city and into Centennial Park where the hairpin bends jolted my knees. Tired, wary of injury, I walked for ten minutes, sipping sports drink and wondering what everyone else in the park made of the marathon pageantry. A bunch of cyclists cut into the marathon course, hollering war chants and stopping the flow. "Go get your fucking lattes!" yelled an angry runner, and I cackled until I was ready to run again.

Finally—eventually, effortfully—I ran down Macquarie Street, through Hyde Park, down the final loop near the Art Gallery and to the finish line. I crossed the line, ready to stop, but really, if I could have kept running like this, everything moving, the world, me, every human within sight, the past within grasp, the future just a few steps ahead, I would have.

I didn't fight my way across the finish line—nor did I float. The significance of that marathon didn't lie in speed or in pain, but in the exchange between my body and the city. I didn't need a personal best trophy; I could prize the run on its own terms. After many years of early morning runs and all kinds of races, running is to me a way of being, not a way of testing myself against invisible antagonists and not a competition with my peers. I had nothing to vanquish but my doubts, and now—in ways I could never have predicted—running has brought me into a rich communion with the world. It still surprises me. I'm careful not to slip on dirt tracks, and I pay more attention to warnings about overstraining my knees than I used to. I want to avoid injury. I don't want a show-stopping finish line moment. I want to keep running.

Conclusion

———————

STORIES WE TELL

I've run a half marathon in Sydney every autumn since I started running. In 2015, I signed up again. It had been a difficult few months; there had been deaths in my family, and I felt dejected, depleted. I'd been unwell too, in the hospital, and my fitness had sunk, although I hadn't altogether lost the habit of running.

Once I would have sought solace in a bottle of gin, my dad's Bessie Smith records, and a bath. Instead, I ran, hoping that some regular rhythm would be restored. I knew that a few longer runs every week would help me sleep better, that having a weird running carnival in my sights would cheer me up. Stress was making me sluggish, and on weekdays I had to talk myself into running as if I were a child: find some clean socks, tie your shoelaces, pull your hair back from your face. I promised myself a hit of adrenaline, drafts of autumn air, the special alertness carried by exertion, and, eventually, a consolatory cup of coffee.

Only the long runs on the weekend were straightforward, and I craved these excursions as the working week ground on. I finished one hot, hilly training run behind golf courses tucked into a green bend of the Brisbane River, and another along the Yarra Trail on a very cold Melbourne morning. In Adelaide, I ran through the manicured Torrens parklands, stopping to peer at the maps posted next to each bridge to make sure I wasn't lost, that I hadn't run too far from my hotel. My fitness returned, or at least some of it, and by May I was ready to run a half marathon.

It used to take me ten minutes to roll down the ridge line of William Street to reach Hyde Park, where the event starts each year. Half awake, I could kid myself that I was just out for another training run. To have made it on time from my new perch on the edge of the city, I would have had to wait for a train on a tiny platform in the quietest pitch of the early morning and then shiver in the shelter for an hour. The cockatoos and koels wouldn't even have woken to shriek their farewells. Instead, I stayed with Anne the night before, and ate mushroom lasagna and couscous with my cousins as their two enormous labradors licked my feet—good luck, everyone agreed.

The next morning, when the sky was still dark, I rose in an unfamiliar house, fumbling for light switches and teaspoons. With a bib pinned to my singlet, I scurried down a shadowy Glebe Point Road to catch a bus into the city—but all the early buses were full of runners, and the drivers shut their doors on me. It began to rain. I quickened my pace and made for Hyde Park on foot, worried that I'd be late, that all this effort was for nothing, as if race day was the only day that mattered. Just as the first wave of runners was leaving, I arrived, caught a hint of warmth in the early light, and relaxed. The drizzle stopped. A Sunday morning in May, and I was waiting outside a sandstone cathedral, ready to take my place in a temporary congregation of runners.

The crowd surged down Macquarie Street into the canyons formed by city buildings. Several thousand runners move through narrow streets as a viscous liquid moves through a funnel. I stayed in the middle of the flow, seeking quick currents forward and avoiding the eddies created by groups determined to take every step together. I ran behind a wide middle-aged man with the face of a smiling child printed on the back of his red shirt. I passed girls with orange and lime-green tutus rustling at their hips, a man in a Batman suit, fathers pushing baby carriages.

The distance slipped by, and it wasn't until I saw the 10-kilometer marker that I started to grumble. I could now recognize this mid-race irritability as a predictable feature of any half marathon. A crisis of confidence and humor would engulf me; a few miles later, my mood would be rolling again. I'd almost reached the point where I looked forward to this stroppiness. The stitch in my stomach I blamed on the mushroom lasagna. The ridges of my socks were digging into my feet, tearing into my flesh. I wished that I was fitter, that I felt light on my feet, that this run, at least, could be uncomplicated. I got stuck behind a drift of tall men who spat so vehemently and so regularly that I didn't dare pass them. Elbows swatted my ribs at the drink stand; the sponsor's electrolyte concoction tasted disgusting, and I could hardly swallow it. A twist of black cherry jellies was in my pocket, and when I sucked one, the sugar jolted me back into action.

The roads were slick after the rain. Over the final few miles, runners around me started to topple. "He went over hard," I heard someone say of a kid on a stretcher. "Look at her. She slipped and hit her head. There's no way she'll make it."

As I approached the finish line I ran alongside a pair of women, both a little older than me, wearing matching singlets and hats of a luscious pink, their faces pulled taut with emotion. One drew her hand to the small of the other's back, as if she were pushing her to the end of the course. "Think of how far you've come," she said. "You're almost there. Let the anger go." It was an intimate exchange to which I was an uneasy witness.

I left the women behind, but I'm sure they both finished the race—and so did I, in a happy tumble of limbs. I know of nothing that's as reliable as running for elevations of mood and emotion, for a sense of self-possession.

*

Later that morning, I sat with my grandfather and traced for him the course I'd just run on a map, as my sister arranged pastries on a plate. We ate the danishes, and I answered his questions about new developments on the harborside and the traffic disruptions caused by the race. Once he was satisfied, he sat back in his chair. "Better you than me," he said—and, after a pause, ruefully added, "I think my running days are over."

Years earlier, I'd set myself the task of running the City-2Surf. It seemed so improbable, I gave no thought to what would happen afterward. I had no premonition that my running days would go on and on, that running would bring me such comfort. When I finished that first race, my grandfather was walking comfortably, playing golf, driving all over town to drink with his friends, keeping the schoolboy slang of the 1930s in circulation. He doesn't get around so much anymore. Me, I am still running.

In Lewis Carroll's *Through the Looking-Glass*, Alice clambers into a world that at first resembles the one she just left. The surfaces of this new reality are soon distorted, and Alice finds herself in the Red Queen's garden conducting curious conversations with the flowers. She frightens uppity daisies, and discusses the niceties of petals and thorns with a rose and a tiger lily. The Queen appears and, once again, the world shifts:

> Alice never could quite make out, in thinking it over afterward, how it was that they began: all she remembers is, that they were running hand in hand, and the Queen went so fast that it was all she could do to keep up with her.

I know how she felt. I used to sit in cafes and pooh-pooh morning runners over my latte. Now, I wonder what they're training for. If I go away to work in another city or on a vacation, I pack my sneakers. The Red Queen explains to Alice: "Now, here, you see, it takes all the running you can do, to keep in the same place. If you want to get somewhere else, you must run at least twice as fast as that!" The boss lady's race sounds like a patriarchal horror treadmill. It reminds me of that old feminist line about Ginger Rogers having to do everything Fred Astaire did, but backward and wearing heels. The

Red Queen isn't making a feminist point, not exactly; she's pointing to the topsy-turvy nature of her world. I've run on both sides of the looking glass, and the rules still don't all make sense to me.

*

My experience as a runner isn't typical—but whose is? The high school cross-country runner who returns to distance running in her thirties? The recently divorced mother who starts to run to help her sleep? The bored gym nut who decides to venture out into the world? The elite athlete who devotes her life to running, who wins marathons and breaks world records?

There are bigger stories about women and running that I've barely brushed in this book. In 2015, Siabatou Sanneh from Gambia walked the Paris Marathon with a bucket of water balanced on her head, drawing attention to the difficulties that women in West Africa face in accessing clean water. My marathons do not resemble hers, and there's also little crossover between my experience and that of women who risk social sanctions to run marathons in Morocco and Pakistan, or that of the East African women who travel the world cleaning up on the competitive circuit. In New York I met young Indigenous women from central Australia, brilliant runners, who were about to take part in the Indigenous Marathon Project established by Robert de Castella.

Middle-class white women like me tend to have an easier run of it, and I know that in dwelling on my own experiences, certain assumptions and exclusions have made their way into this book. Maybe the only thing we all have in common, as women, is that we've been told we shouldn't run this far, that we should slow down, be careful. When I look at the women runners around me, I don't see the restrictions we've been told we must accept—I see extraordinary diversity.

Women who run: women with disabilities, fat women, women who've recovered from physical injuries, trans women, migrant women, Indigenous women, depressed women, women with no time, women with no kids, ladies of leisure, schoolgirls, retirees, mothers, aunts, grandmothers, queer women, straight women, slow women. Scrutinize any one of these categories and a set of stories that defy generalization will emerge, stories that destabilize the big stupid myths that say women can't run, that only certain kinds of women can run, that it's too dangerous, that it's unfeminine, that it's a sign of trouble.

Not one of the women waiting to start the half marathon in Hyde Park knew that I was casting her in an ensemble piece about the many ways women run, that I was ready to listen to the quiet stories her feet might drum about endurance and the bloody marvels of human biology. If I'd taken a survey, each woman would have had something different to say about running—and many, I'm sure, would have disputed the claims I've made about the sport. "I've never felt scared running alone at night," one of the ladies in the pink shirts might have said, and her friend could have added, "I can't think of anything more romantic than one of those big trackside marriage proposals. Also, waterproof mascara makes me feel great."

I didn't plan to write a book about running that drew quite so much on my own trajectory as a runner. How else, though, could I ground my objection to the stock portraits of women who run? I turned my gaze away from the medal winners, the damsels in distress, the renegades, the really fast runners, and looked into the mirror. There was a runner I could write about.

Now, the great breach between my running self and the nonrunner I believed myself to be has narrowed. Strength and energy ripple through a body that I'd been told was weak. I've spewed up all the cultural toxins that made me so sure that it was just me—with my wonky, wobbly legs and overdeveloped self-consciousness—who couldn't run. I know I'm not the only person to have kidded herself like this. I might not have become a champion, but I've become a runner, and somewhere along the way I stopped raging about what my life might have been like if that plane hadn't crashed. That's a life that I can now see has been plotted by surprises: including both an horrific plane crash and the discovery of contentment in running. I've been fit enough to run marathons and, in between, I have slowed down and sped up again, delighted by my body's capacity for renewal. There are many limits to my progress as a runner: some of them lie within me, some are beyond my control. Instead of trying to master the contingencies, I just live with them.

Grief is no longer so strange to my peers; many have now endured the kinds of loss that are rare to twenty-year-olds. Had my parents died when I was thirty-five, I wouldn't have felt so alone. I know now that some people go into paroxysms over the death of a distant relative, and that others sit quietly with their hurt for years. I've watched friends assiduously confront grief and return to life with determination, only to find themselves helpless when the pain surges again. The lonely specifics of loss can rarely be dressed in off-the-rack narratives. Grief leaves people confused, self-destructive, lost to themselves—at least for a while—far more often than it creates heroes. If someone has a sad story to tell, I listen, because no story is sadder than the one that goes unheard. Were a melancholy person to ask my advice, I'd tell her that running moved me, restored to me my vigor—then I'd remember that in my grimmest moments, I would have lashed with fury the proposal that I go running. When I run, I'm reminded that lives can change and habits can be broken, that movement can simultaneously be metaphor and action.

*

I now run on the sidewalks by roads that cling to the coastline between Sydney and Wollongong. When I visit my grandfather, I sometimes run around Balmain, Leichhardt, Five Dock, and Drummoyne and afterward, I sit with him on his balcony, watching the boats hum between Drummoyne and Hunters Hill. I run on rocky tracks on the Illawarra Escarpment and on fire trails through dry eucalypts in the Royal National Park. When I can, I return to my old routes around the waterfront, through the Botanical Gardens, across the Bridge. When I'm busy in the city, I run in the gym at the university where I work, and I watch the news on a tiny treadmill screen with headphones twisted into my ears. Usually I run on my own, close to rivers, lakes, and oceans, as if to draw replenishment from the water and comfort from the great skies that emerge from them.

The weekend after that last Sydney half marathon, I found myself away from home again. I woke before dawn in Canberra and drove to the National Gallery so that I could watch the sun rise from within a room built by the artist James Turrell. Out of the darkness, the sky bloomed yellow, pink, and blue.

When it was light enough to run, I set out on the path that circles Lake Burley Griffin. The last time I'd run there, I had mucked up that marathon. The temperature hovered at zero: my ungloved hands were painfully cold, and my throat burned on each inhalation. Heavy banks of mist rose from the water; garnet-colored leaves caught the first morning sunlight; galahs dug for seeds in grasslands rigid with frost; yellow poplars blazed alongside conifers and eucalypts I couldn't name; hot-air balloons floated from the horizon at the opposite bank. I ran to stay warm and I ran to buoy my mood and I ran to stay a part of this glorious composition. I ran too because once I'd committed to the loop, I had no other way of getting back to my car. That morning I ran 13 miles, and my pace was much faster than it had been in the half marathon I'd completed the week before.

I don't know where I'll run my next race, but I do know—at least as I write these lines—that I'll go out for a run on the weekend, that my pulse will rush, that along the way, or maybe when I'm back at home, sitting on the front step, pulling at my shoelaces, the sky will appear brighter and the water that I drink to quench my thirst will seem extraordinarily clear.

BIBLIOGRAPHY

Aaken, Ernst van. "Van Aaken Method." *Runner's World*, 1976.

ABC Online, "24-hour disappearance of 18yo Bendigo jogger an 'horrendous' ordeal, parents say." ABC Online, August 3, 2015. http://www.abc.net.au/news/2015-08-02/family-18yo-jogger-appeals-for-privacy-after-horrendous-ordeal/6666442.

Algeo, Matthew. "Pedestrianism: When Watching People Walk Was America's Favorite Spectator Sport." *Chicago Review Press*, 2014.

Aubusson, Kate. "Women who walk alone at night invite predators, says mayor of Albury after alleged rape." *Sydney Morning Herald*, May 1, 2015.

Battista, Garth, ed. *The Runner's Literary Companion: Great Stories and Poems about Running.* Penguin, 1996.

Baudrillard, Jean. *America.* Translated by Chris Turner. Verso, 1989.

Boccaccio, Giovanni. *The Decameron.* Translated by John Payne. Walter Black, c. 1890.

Bowerman, William J., and W. E. Harris, *Jogging.* Corgi, 1968.

Brant, John; Andy Milroy; Kevin Kelly; Peter Lovesey; and Alex Wilson. "Did Violet Piercy run a valid 3:40:22 marathon in 1926?" *Track Stats*, May 2009.

Browning, Robert. *The Complete Works of Robert Browning: Dramatic Idylls: I and II.* Ohio University Press, 2007.

Carter, Ron. "Adrienne makes short work of the marathon." *The Age*, September 1, 1971.

Carver, Raymond. *What We Talk about When We Talk about Love.* Vintage, 1981.

Cook, Henrietta. "Girls at Islamic school banned from running, teachers claim." *The Age*, April 23, 2015.

Cooper, Kenneth H. *Aerobics.* Bantam, 1968.

Coubertin, Pierre de. *Olympism: Selected Writings.* International Olympic Committee, 2000.

D'Ambrosio, Charles. *Loitering: New and Collected Essays.* Tin House, 2014.

Davis, David. *Marathon Crasher: The Life and Times of Merry Lepper, the First American Woman to Run a Marathon.* Thomas Dunne Books, 2012.

Didion, Joan. "New York: Sentimental journeys." *New York Review of Books*, January 17, 1991.

Foster Wallace, David. *Infinite Jest.* Little, Brown, 1996.

Friedan, Betty. *The Feminine Mystique.* Norton, 1963.

Gibb, Bobbi. *To Boston with Love: The Story of the First Woman to Run the Boston Marathon.* Gibb Art Works, 1980.

Giddings, Caitlin. "The Trailblazer: Arlene Pieper." *Runner's World*, December 10, 2013.

Gilbert, Sandra M., and Susan Gubar. *The Madwoman in the Attic: The Woman Writer and the Nineteenth-Century Literary Imagination.* Yale University Press, 1979.

Gilmour, Garth. *Run for Your Life: Jogging with Arthur Lydiard.* Minerva, 1965.

Gotaas, Thor. *Running: A Global History.* Reaktion, 2009.

Graves, Robert. *The Greek Myths.* Penguin Classics, 1955.

Gross, Albert C. *Endurance: The Events, The Athletes, The Attitude.* Dodd, Mead and Co., 1986.

Hansen, Jacqueline. *A Long Time Coming: Running through the Women's Marathon Revolution.* CreateSpace, 2013.

Heinrich, Bernd. *Why We Run: A Natural History.* Ecco, 2002.

Hinds, Alex. "'Matildas' pay dispute: Gallop promises new deal will lift women to 'professional' status." *Guardian* Australia, October 16, 2015. http://www.theguardian.com/football/2015/oct/16/matildas -pay-dispute-ffa-gallop-professional-status.

Jutel, Anne-Marie. "Forgetting Millie Sampson: Collective Frameworks for Historical Memory," *New Zealand Journal of Media Studies*, Volume 10 (1), 2007.

Kostrubala, Thaddeus. *The Joy of Running.* Lippincott, 1976.

Krise, Raymond, and Bill Squires. *Fast Tracks: The History of Distance Running Since 884 B.C.* The Stephen Greene Press, 1982.

Lambros Sp. P., and N. G. Polites. *The Olympic Games: B.C. 776–A.D. 1896.* H.G. Grevel, 1896.

Lander, Christian. "#27: Marathons," *Stuff White People Like.* http:// stuffwhitepeoplelike.com/2008/01/26/27-marathons.

Leigh, Mary H., and Thérèse M. Bonin. "The Pioneering Role of Madame Alice Milliat and the FSFI in Establishing International Track and Field Competition for Women." *Journal of Sports History*, Volume 4 (1), 1972.

Lennartz, Karl. "Two Women Ran the Marathon in 1896," *Citius, Altius, Fortius*, Volume 2 (1), Winter 1994.

Lovesey, Peter. "Violet Piercy (b. 1889?)," *Oxford Dictionary of National Biography*, first published May 2012.

Lydiard, Arthur, with Garth Gilmour. *Jogging with Lydiard.* Hodder and Stoughton, 1983.

"The Marathon: Physiological, Medical, Epidemiological, and Psychological Studies." *Annals of the New York Academy of Sciences*, Volume 301, October 1977.

McDougall, Christopher. *Born to Run: A Hidden Tribe, Superathletes, and the Greatest Race the World Has Never Seen.* Vintage, 2009.

Messerli, D. F. M. *Women's Participation in the Modern Olympic Games. Report to the International Olympic Committee.* International Olympic Committee, 1952.

Mill, J. S. *Collected Works.* Edited by J. M. Robson. University of Toronto Press, 1978.

Miller, Tristan. *Run Like Crazy.* Penguin, 2012.

Miragaya, Ana. "The Female Olympian: Tradition versus Innovation in the Quest for Inclusion." In Lamartine P. DaCosta, ed., *Olympic Studies: Current Intellectual Crossroads.* Editora Gama Filho, 2002.

Murakami, Haruki. *What I Talk about When I Talk about Running.* Vintage, 2007.

Oates, Joyce Carol. "To invigorate literary mind, start moving literary feet." *The New York Times,* July 18, 1999.

O'Neill, Maureen, and Angie Calder. "Cutting down the tall poppies: Female athletes bullied in Aussie schools." *The Conversation,* July 21, 2015. https://theconversation.com/cutting-down-the-tall-poppies -female-athletes-bullied-in-aussie-schools-44223.

Radford, Peter. "Women's Foot-Races in the 18th and 19th Centuries: A Popular and Widespread Practice." *Canadian Journal of History of Sport,* Volume 25 (1), 1994.

Robinson, Roger. *Running in Literature: A Guide for Scholars, Readers, Runners, Joggers and Dreamers.* Breakaway Books, 2003.

Rogin, Gilbert. "The Fastest Is Faster." *Sports Illustrated,* October 5, 1964.

Schultz, Jaime. "Going the Distance: The Road to the 1984 Olympic Women's Marathon." *International Journal of the History of Sport,* Volume 32 (1), 2015.

Sears, Edward S. *Running through the Ages.* McFarland, 2001.

Serano, Julia. *Whipping Girl: A Transsexual Woman on Sexism and the Scapegoating of Femininity.* Seal Press, 2007.

Sheehan, George. *Dr. Sheehan on Running.* Bantam, 1975.

———. *Running & Being: The Total Experience.* Rodale, 1978.

———. *Personal Best: The Foremost Philosopher of Fitness Shares Techniques and Tactics for Success and Self-Liberation.* Rodale, 1989.

Shrake, Edwin. "A Lonely Tribe of Long-Distance Runners," *Sports Illustrated*, January 9, 1967, as quoted in Nina Kuscsik, "The History of Women's Participation in the Marathon," speech to the National Women's Long Distance Running Committee, 1977.

Sillitoe, Alan. *The Loneliness of the Long-Distance Runner.* Vintage, 1959.

Steele, Richard. *Poetical Miscellanies: Consisting of Original Poems and Translations by the Best Hands.* Jacob Tonson, 1714.

Switzer, Kathrine. *Marathon Woman.* Carroll & Graf, 2007.

Tarasouleas, Athanasios. "Stamata Revithi, 'Alias Melpomeni.'" *Sport and Women*, 1997.

Walker, Donald. *Exercises for Ladies Calculated to Preserve and Improve Beauty.* T. Hurst, 1857.

Young, Iris Marion. "Throwing Like a Girl: A Phenomenology of Feminine Body Comportment Motility and Spatiality," *Human Studies*, Volume 3 (2), April 1980.

ACKNOWLEDGMENTS

Running might be a solo undertaking but I haven't written this book on my own. There are many people I'd like to thank for their help in getting this manuscript over the line. Firstly, I'd like to acknowledge the good people at Affirm Press, who took a punt on this project, especially Kate Goldsworthy and Martin Hughes, along with Lyn Tranter and Aviva Tuffield. I'd like to thank Meghan Houser for patiently steering *The Long Run* to U.S. publication.

I know I've come close to being a running bore over the years and I'm indebted to all the friends and strangers who have endured my soliloquys on marathons. I'm grateful to those who have talked with me about the ideas in this book and read sections of the manuscript: Ben Allen, Ed Barnes, Jasmine Bruce, Jim Casey, Jarrah Ekstein, Bruce Gardiner, Melissa Gregg, Cait Harris, Jocelyn Hungerford, Adrian Jones,

Emma Kearney, Sean Kelly, Rachel Maher, Leah McLennan, Miranda Nagy, Kate O'D, Rachel O'Reilly, Todd Packer, Alecia Simmonds, Damian Spruce, Dan Stacey, Jason Wilson, Geordie Williamson, Alex Wregg, Emma Young.

Thanks to my Albury training advisers: Prue, Tony, Meg and Tess Smith. Thanks too to the speedy Elder tribe for the training advice, the racing company, and all the running yarns: Ali and Anna; Danny and Phoebe; Laurie and Elle; Mads and Jamie—and, of course, to Anne Pike, for all that and more.

I may never convert my three sisters to running but together they form a fabulous cheering squad: thanks to Lucy Pike and Claudia Robbins for patient enthusiasm; I couldn't do without the encouragement I receive from Laura Pike in running, writing, and life. My grandfather Bruce Menzies has inquired about the progress of this book at least once a week for several years. I'm lucky to have such a staunch supporter, and, like him, I'm relieved that it's finally complete. My partner Daniel Heckenberg has sustained me through the writing of this book, through many long and short runs; I thank him for his love and companionship.

And finally, I'd like to thank my mum and dad, to whom writing this book has brought me closer. I wish they'd had the chance to read it.

ABOUT THE AUTHOR

Credit: Daniel Heckenberg

Catriona Menzies-Pike is the editor of the *Sydney Review of Books*. Her career in online media includes stints as the managing editor of the pioneering news and current affairs website New Matilda and as arts editor of *The Conversation*. She's taught literature, film, journalism, and cultural studies to undergraduates across Sydney since 2001. In 2007 she ran her first half marathon and she's been running ever since.